MW00559430

Knowledge Management Basics

Christee Gabour Atwood

PRESS

Alexandria, Virginia

A. MURILLO

ASTD Press is an internationally renowned source of insightful and practical information on workplace learning and performance topics, including training basics, evaluation and return on investment, instructional systems development, e-learning, leadership, and career development.

Ordering information: Books published by ASTD Press can be purchased by visiting ASTD's website at store.astd.org or by calling 800.628.2783 or 703.683.8100.

Library of Congress Control Number: 2008928317

ISBN-10: 1-56286-548-X
ISBN-13: 978-1-56286-548-1

ASTD Press Editorial Staff:

Director: Dean Smith
Manager, Acquisitions and Author Relations: Mark Morrow
Editorial Manager: Jacqueline Edlund-Braun
Senior Associate Editor: Tora Estep
Editorial Assistant: Georgina Del Priore

Copyeditor: Christine Cotting
Indexer: April Davis
Proofreader: Appingo
Interior Design and Production: UpperCase Publication Services, Ltd.
Cover Design: Ana Ilieva Foreman
Cover Illustration: D.M. Grethen

Printed by Versa Press, Inc., East Peoria, Illinois; www.versapress.com

Contents

About the
Training Basics Series

▪ ▪

A STD's *Training Basics* series recognizes and, in some ways, celebrates the fast-paced, ever-changing reality of organizations today. Jobs, roles, and expectations change quickly. One day you might be a network administrator or a process line manager, and the next day you might be asked to train 50 employees in basic computer skills or to instruct line workers in quality processes.

Where do you turn for help? The ASTD *Training Basics* series is designed to be your one-stop solution. The series takes a minimalist approach to your learning curve dilemma and presents only the information you need to be successful. Each book in the series guides you through key aspects of training: giving presentations, making the transition to the role of trainer, designing and delivering training, and evaluating training. The books in the series also include some advanced skills such as performance and basic business proficiencies.

The ASTD *Training Basics* series is the perfect tool for training and performance professionals looking for easy-to-understand materials that will prepare nontrainers to take on a training role. In addition, this series is the perfect reference tool for any trainer's bookshelf and a quick way to hone your existing skills.

Preface

Is the thought of capturing every bit of knowledge in your organization, validating it, categorizing it, and putting it in a format that everyone can use enough to make you crawl under your desk and stay there? The work sounds overwhelming. But as this book takes you through the process, you will discover that effectively managing organizational knowledge is not as daunting a task as you first might imagine.

When you understand key concepts and know what tools and resources are available or easily constructed, and when we've walked step-by-step through the process outlined in this book, you'll be ready not only to ask the right questions to elicit needed information, but also to help your organization set up the basic framework to accomplish what you initially thought impossible—capturing and using the most valuable knowledge for business advantage. More important, you will discover how your role as a workplace learning professional intersects with the complex body of organizational systems, processes, and the people who must understand and use corporate knowledge to create business value.

There are very significant bottom-line costs for an organization that doesn't use its stores of institutional knowledge and doesn't take advantage of the valuable information its employees have. Helping you avoid those assaults on the bottom line is one of my priorities in writing this book. I want to explain knowledge management (KM) to you, describe how to find and gather what your organization knows, and give you tools and techniques to use in formatting and communicating that knowledge. Just as important, this book offers ways your organization can keep the scope of its knowledge management system *manageable* so that every person involved—including the learning function—can perform his or her roles successfully.

Finally, in this *Basics* book you will learn about the importance of effective communication in any knowledge management system—a core competency for all learning professionals. Sharing ideas and best practices will build both support for and investment in knowledge management systems, no matter how simple or how intricate they are.

Who Should Read This Book?

This book is designed to give an overview that will help individuals at all levels of the organization understand the benefits and basic framework of knowledge management systems. For the human resource professional, the book reviews the role that KM can play in orienting new employees and retaining the current workforce because of the increased job satisfaction that comes from having the tools and information needed to do the required work. Organization development personnel will be able to use this as a reference to visualize the acceleration KM can bring to their efforts by opening communication and discovering processes that can be made more effective. And executives and managers will appreciate a better understanding of the savings KM can create for the bottom line through effective use and sharing of information.

As a learning professional, you are in the business of sharing information—perhaps even making many of the vital corporate connections that create organizational value through the sharing of knowledge. This book will help you take a deliberate role in any enterprise-wide effort to harness the power of corporate knowledge.

A Chapter-by-Chapter Look Through the Book

One of the absolute values of this book is its focus on simplicity—after all, it is a *Basics* book. This means that complex theory (which clearly has its value) is saved for your graduate study. Here we focus on helping you "get your head around" what needs to be done and the key players who need to do it.

Knowledge management is delivered in a variety of formats; and the term itself has been used to describe computer systems, information databases, and even the individuals who preserve information in an organization. The first chapter—"What Is Knowledge Management?"—defines the current use of the term and identifies the basic concepts of managing knowledge. Additionally, it outlines the five steps that are necessary to implement a universal system of knowledge management in an organization.

In chapter 2, "How Organizations Are Using KM," the focus is on the reasons why organizations are finding KM necessary for the growth and efficient operations of their businesses. It looks at specific examples of challenges and how those situations were improved by the effective sharing of knowledge. Also discussed are the elements of collecting and disseminating knowledge that are in all successful KM systems. The chapter also presents ways to garner support for a KM system in your organization and ways to maintain that momentum once the program has been in place for an extended period of time.

Chapter 3 is titled "Determining Your Organization's KM Goals and Needs." Gathering large amounts of knowledge in a database is not the ultimate goal of a KM system. It's how that knowledge is made available, shared, and built on that determines the ultimate success and continuation of the system. This chapter discusses setting specific KM system business objectives that are tied directly to the organization's goals. It also investigates ways to discover an organization's needs through auditing of current knowledge sources, detecting frequently needed knowledge, and discovering the gaps that exist between the two.

Chapter 4, "Locating Information Sources in Your Organization," discusses one of the first tasks in knowledge management: discovering the most important knowledge sources in the organization. No matter the size or complexity of your organization, there are stores of knowledge—many of them hidden in plain sight—in overlooked or underused employees (such as subject matter experts) and in ignored or forgotten documents and processes. This chapter outlines methods to discover the typical documented forms of knowledge that exist and recommends methods to retain the wisdom and practices that may be lost when seasoned employees leave the organization.

Chapter 5 is titled "Creating Your KM Blueprint." The knowledge that is available to members of an organization is only useful if it is actually *used*. This chapter reviews the formats for collecting existing knowledge and making it accessible to the workforce through a single access point to ensure that workers always retrieve the most current information. It also discusses the social and networking opportunities that allow the accumulation of new knowledge through discussion and sharing of best practices so that the knowledge base continues to grow.

When the format of the KM system has been defined, the knowledge that will occupy the system must be processed. Chapter 6, "Compiling, Confirming, and Circulating the Knowledge," addresses that issue. Compiling the knowledge will be accomplished through various methods, depending on the form in which the information exists—documents, databases, notes, or even in the heads of valued employees. The chapter then discusses the checks and balances of confirming that information in accordance with company policies, processes, and procedures. Finally, the rollout of the system—the circulating of the knowledge housed there—is described.

"Maintaining the KM System" is the focus of chapter 7. In the final step of the five-step process of developing a system to manage an organization's knowledge, the knowledge should be considered a product to be reviewed and improved on continually. Just as a product distributed to external customers is evaluated and upgraded time and again, the knowledge housed in a KM system must be monitored regularly to maintain its integrity and value. If users access information that is outdated or incomplete, confidence in the system will erode and its use will decrease. This chapter outlines follow-up activities to monitor the KM data, methods and measurements to evaluate its level of success, and potential areas for expansion and revision as the KM system becomes embedded in the organizational culture.

Chapter 8, "KM Resources and Tools," considers what's available to make the KM process more effective. Although software systems and communication advancements are occurring at such a rate as to make specific KM product reviews obsolete a moment after they're written, there are specific resources and features that can be considered when looking at any KM tool. This chapter poses questions to ask and elements to consider in designing a KM system. It also includes forms that will help in the collection of knowledge and tools that will help convey an understanding of KM and its concepts and benefits to members of the organization.

Chapter 9, "Best Practices in KM," offers you an opportunity to learn from organizations that currently use KM systems. No KM effort is completely successful in its first phase. There always are adjustments to be made, specific company culture and needs to be addressed, and other factors that must be taken into consideration. By studying other companies' successes and areas of challenge, this chapter gives you the benefits of their lessons learned as you and the KM project team pursue your own KM initiative.

Chapter 10 looks at "The Future of KM" for your organization. One feature that is necessary to every KM system is flexibility. The system must be evaluated and revised to answer current organizational needs and to reflect updates in the information. It should be upgraded to incorporate the newest advances in the organization's communication methods. And it should be redesigned as needed to accommodate the end users' preferences. This chapter focuses on addressing these needs while consistently observing the basic KM principles. This section also considers the future expansion of your organization's KM system.

In Appendix A, you'll discover communication points to help convey the benefits and processes of a KM initiative for your organization. It includes brief answers to frequently asked questions that will help others understand the potential advancements in communication and efficiency of processes that are possible when knowledge is expanded and shared. Appendix B is a script you may use in conjunction with the PowerPoint slide presentation discussed in chapter 8. Finally, the Resources section suggests numerous places to learn more about knowledge management.

Look for These Icons

This book tries to make it easy for you to understand and apply its lessons. The following icons used throughout the book will help you zoom in on key points:

What's Inside This Chapter?

Each chapter opens with a summary of the topics covered in it. You can use this list to find the areas that interest you most.

Basic Rules

These rules cut to the chase. They represent important concepts and assumptions that form the foundation of a knowledge management effort in your organization.

Think About This

These are helpful tips for how to use the tools and techniques presented and ancillary information about the topics covered in the chapter.

Noted

This icon offers other experts' perspectives and ideas on knowledge management and communication.

Getting It Done

The final section of each chapter offers action steps, suggestions, additional resources, or questions to help you put what you've learned in the chapter to use in your organization.

Acknowledgments

I did not write this book alone. This was truly a joint effort with the help of an incredibly supportive ASTD editorial staff; Mark Morrow, manager of acquisitions and author relations at ASTD Press; and, finally, the diligent efforts of the unsinkable Christine Cotting, our editor on this group project.

I realized that this project wasn't a solo effort for the same reason that knowledge management itself can't be an individual undertaking. In fact, many of the challenges that are identified in this book are the same ones I encountered while sifting through the massive amounts of information and varying viewpoints on knowledge management.

I found myself asking questions such as

▶ Which of these pieces of knowledge are vital to understanding the topic?
▶ Which practices are the most current?
▶ What are the success stories and the mistakes we can learn from?

▶ How much information is too much?

▶ What's the best format for this material?

All of these are the questions a KM initiative must consider. And I found that one person can't always answer every question effectively. It takes a team united by a specific goal and a shared vision to make a KM project success-ful—or, in this case, to make a KM book.

My thanks and gratitude to an incredible team.

–Christee Gabour Atwood
April 2009

1

What Is Knowledge Management?

What's Inside This Chapter

In this chapter, you'll learn

▶ The definition of knowledge management
▶ The key concepts of managing knowledge
▶ How the learning professional participates in a knowledge management initiative
▶ The steps to implementing your knowledge management system.

earning professionals have been hearing an abundance of conflicting information about knowledge management, so let's start here with a discussion designed to clear up a few misconceptions:

▶ Knowledge management (KM) is not a new concept. As individuals, we've been building on knowledge learned all our lives. As nations and as a world community, we turn to history books for knowledge about the past so we don't have to keep repeating mistakes or reinventing the same implements and programs. And when we've gathered knowledge, we've begun to manage it—sometimes unconsciously, sometimes quite deliberately—to make the best use of what we do know and to identify what we don't know.

▶ Even in a work environment where technology informs and powers almost everything, KM is not dependent on a software system. Software can make it easier to manage knowledge, but it's not a prerequisite for starting to think of ways to capture and build on the expertise in an organization.

▶ KM is not a one-time event. It is an ongoing process that requires continual maintenance if it is not to become obsolete.

▶ KM is not the possession of any one department. Although the expertise of individuals such as the organization's learning professionals is vital to its success, the entire project of creating a KM system is best served by a cross-departmental team, and maintenance of the system is an organizationwide responsibility.

So, if knowledge management is not any of the items listed above, then exactly what is it? Here's a brief definition of the concept at work in an organization:

Managing knowledge is identifying useful knowledge that exists in the organization and making it available to others to use or build on.

Think About This

A number of terms have appeared for the concept of *knowledge management*. Among the variations are *knowledge sharing, information management, knowledge focus, environment management, knowledge capture systems, idea sharing, knowledge integration, knowledge mobilization,* and *intellectual asset management*. However, the term *knowledge management* is most widely recognized at this time.

Think About This

With the impending retirement of the post-WWII Boomer Generation, knowledge management is becoming a priority as organizations realize the importance of capturing the knowledge and wisdom of those individuals before they leave.

That's it. Yes, many detailed explanations exist, but that definition captures the essential aspects of all KM initiatives and processes.

Organizations are built on knowledge—history, successes, failures, research, the experiences of individual employees—and being able to use that knowledge effectively and to build on it creates organizations' specific strategic advantages. Each organization generates and uses information specific to its industry and its function in the marketplace (for example, proprietary formulas or recipes, competitor research, and marketing strategies); at the same time, all organizations compile and use employee and customer contact information, lists of suppliers, operational guides, and department policies and procedures manuals. This knowledge creates the foundation of a KM system.

This foundation becomes a system through a collaboration that typically involves key positions, including senior management representatives who ensure that the KM system is aligned with the organization's business goals; learning professionals who use the principles of training transfer to help design the system; information technology (IT) representatives who will determine what systems are required to support KM needs; and departmental representatives who not only find subject matter experts to confirm knowledge, but also help determine the best ways to package the information for their department's end users of the KM system.

The benefits of KM for the average employee can best be identified by comparison to the ultimate knowledge management tool—the Internet. It's a vast, constantly expanding source of virtually any information an individual could need. But knowing that this resource exists and not having a way to search and retrieve relevant information easily would make this remarkable tool more frustrating than useful. Fortunately, search engines have created a gateway for the average person to access the information available on the Internet. A KM system for an organization offers the same service by creating a gateway that the average worker will use to access organizational knowledge, to submit questions to subject matter experts, or even to find communities that address his or her specific needs. These contacts may be online, through training opportunities, one-on-one, or in company documents, but regardless of their format, the knowledge will be accessed through a single gateway so the employee knows he or she is getting the most up-to-date information on the topic.

Who's Using KM, and Why?

During the 1990s, many U.S. federal, state, and local government agencies were mandated to adopt electronic information systems intended to capture and use the knowledge the agencies held. The systems created a need for basic information management processes, and many of those processes became the foundations of current KM practice in the private sector. Following the government's lead, corporations such as Chevron, Dow Chemical, IBM Global Services, and Best Buy, as well as many other large and small corporate entities, invested millions of dollars in bringing these systems onboard. Networks and communities of practice developed, company intranets and extranets expanded to house the knowledge and make it more easily accessible, and portals were created to enable customers to search the company's consumer information directly. The business return on these investments included not only savings in time and money, but also reduced paper use and improved customer satisfaction scores.

Companies have reported the following additional benefits of implementing KM systems:

▶ Streamlined operations and reduced costs resulted from eliminating redundant processes.
▶ Reduced response time improved customer service and satisfaction.
▶ Increased revenues were generated by getting products and services to market faster and more efficiently.
▶ Employee retention rates improved when the value of employees' knowledge was recognized and they were acknowledged or rewarded for it.

▶ New channels for the free flow of ideas nurtured creativity and promoted innovation.

Public knowledge-sharing systems, retail industries' product information portals, learning management systems implemented at the college/university level, and the structured information-sharing practices of the military all have prompted companies to discover their vast stores of knowledge along with ways to circulate this information among employees and sometimes to customers.

Think About This

Take time to list the advantages your organization could experience through the improved sharing of knowledge. Compare these to problem areas, such as low customer service ratings, high employee turnover, and duplication of efforts. Use this information as a foundation for your report on the potential effects of knowledge management for your organization.

The Learning Professional's Role

All learning professionals are knowledge officers, regularly participating in knowledge management. If you've created a step-by-step guide for a process and given it to a work team, if you've directed an employee to an operations manual to find an answer to a question, or if you've sent an email to explain a procedural change, you were practicing knowledge management. Part of your job always has been finding, organizing, and dispersing organizational information. You intuitively understand the big-picture benefits of sharing knowledge both for those employed by your organization and for customers.

Although knowledge management doesn't belong exclusively to the members of any single department, learning professionals have a spot at the forefront of any KM initiative. When your organization decides to take deliberate steps to create a KM process (perhaps with a department dedicated to it and an executive-level officer or team in charge of it), the new system of gathering, organizing, and sharing information neither diminishes your role nor does it demand that you change the core of what you're doing now. When the new system is in place, you'll continue to gather, organize, and share information to enhance the efficiency and effectiveness of each member of the organization. But with an organizationwide systematic approach to collecting and archiving existing expertise, you'll be able to tap a deeper well of knowledge, and do it more easily. You'll make vital knowledge connections among various pockets of expertise and create a vastly expanded training library that all people in the organization can access, confirm, and build on.

As a learning professional, your main roles in organizational KM are to take part in the initiative to identify knowledge and build communication channels that share and update that knowledge and then to train and encourage others to use the newly created KM systems and processes. As your organization pursues the initiative, you'll be called on to participate in some or all of the following activities:

- researching current knowledge systems in your organization and assisting in the decision-making process to choose systems that will house and disseminate organizational knowledge
- speaking for the KM system as your understanding and appreciation of its benefits grow
- serving as facilitator and trainer in the implementation of new systems and processes designed to manage organizational knowledge
- acting as change agent and even cheerleader to keep employees focused on and excited about using the new system.

Remember that your partners in any KM initiative likely will include people from across the organization—technology representatives, department specialists, and both upper and middle managers. And if channels are planned for customer use too, you'll be working with customer service professionals and representative customers as well.

The Steps to Implementing KM

This book follows the five basic steps in any KM initiative. Understanding these steps will help you (1) define your role in knowledge management efforts and (2) prepare to take a leadership position in the initiative. Figure 1-1 presents an overview of the five-step KM process. The initiative begins with research to identify the organization's needs and is complete when a process

Figure 1-1. Five Steps of Knowledge Management

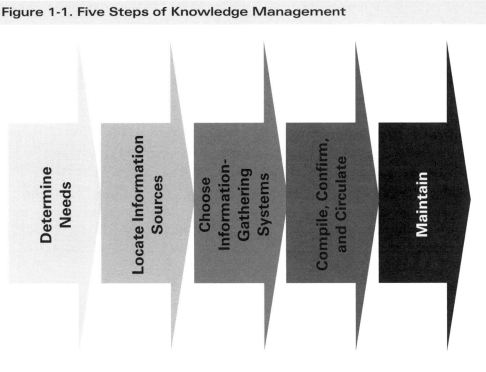

for maintaining the completed system is in place. Here's an overview of the five steps:

1. *Determine the Organization's Needs.* To get anywhere, you have to know where you are and decide where you want to be. It's the same here. At this point, the organization believes it has knowledge that isn't being used effectively or that may be lost to retirement, downsizing, or simple forgetting. It also believes that knowledge is valuable, useful, and worth saving. This is when the learning professional's understanding of instructional design will be vital. The same needs analysis process that initiates training design also serves as the starting point for knowledge management.

2. *Locate Knowledge Sources.* At this point, the team that's working on the KM initiative must identify areas of knowledge and locate subject matter experts, information resources, and documents that already

exist in the organization, as well as probable sources of important unwritten wisdom. The learning professional will be able to call on those same operations and product specialists he or she uses for validation of training information to serve as resources and to help identify others who have access to the most current information.

3. *Choose Systems to Gather and House Information.* When it has identified where knowledge can be captured, the team is better equipped to select methods to use in gathering and storing the knowledge. In this phase of the initiative, you serve as one of the knowledge experts charged with identifying the best ways to gather knowledge, validate it, organize it, and store it so that it is accessible to those who need it. Your role is vital in the process of selecting the solutions that best suit your organization's needs, culture, and technology capabilities.

4. *Compile, Confirm, and Circulate Knowledge.* In this phase, the knowledge is gathered from the identified sources; placed in whatever formats or databases have been chosen for storage; and forwarded to the experts, authorities, and learning professionals to confirm, correct, or expand on. When they have established that the material is accurate and up to date, it's made accessible to whomever will benefit from it.

5. *Maintain the Knowledge System.* Because knowledge is dynamic and always changing, the system that stores and disseminates it must allow easy updating whenever needed. Establishing system ownership and an ongoing maintenance plan is key to success. The learning professional may be the coordinator of the process, or this could be a separate role that the organization develops, such as a chief knowledge officer.

Basic Rule 1

To be effective, knowledge management must address three essential components—people, process, and technology.

Getting It Done

Think about and answer these questions:

1. Do you see gaps and lost opportunities in the way your organization manages knowledge?
2. How do you see your role in creating a KM system for your organization?
3. Is your organization structured to use its expertise fully?
4. How might you position yourself to take a leadership role in a KM initiative?
5. If you were in charge of a KM initiative, how might you go about implementing the five steps briefly discussed in this chapter?

2

How Organizations
Are Using KM

What's Inside This Chapter

In this chapter, you'll learn

▶ Why organizations need to manage knowledge
▶ What elements make up successful KM systems
▶ How your organization can support a KM initiative.

Organizations are deciding to use KM to discover, classify, and validate the knowledge of their employees in answer to essential business needs, such as

- ▶ retention of the expertise and wisdom of personnel
- ▶ acceleration of learning and implementation of new standards, processes, and information
- ▶ increased profits from eliminating duplication of efforts and improving existing processes

▶ improvement of ability to make leadership decisions based on historical and practical experiences

▶ increased customer satisfaction from more efficient processes and consistency of information they receive from customer service representatives

▶ shortened product development time from building on prior successes

▶ collaboration on projects by team members in distant locations.

These business needs are a few of the reasons why organizations may realize they have to discover and organize the knowledge of their employees. These reasons often are discovered through a single query or request that prompts the question, "Why isn't this information readily available?" That was precisely the case in the situation encountered by the U.S. Army's Combined Joint Task Force 76.

This example from the August 2008 Knowledge Management Section report of the U.S. Department of the Army outlines the task force's knowledge-sharing issue and how KM was used to improve operations.

Think About This

The need for sharing knowledge is not isolated to business and industry. Government agencies, nonprofit organizations, universities, and even the military are discovering the benefits of organizing and coordinating knowledge assets to reduce duplication, avoid access to outdated information, and shorten the time of search and retrieve functions.

Case Study: U.S. Combined Joint Task Force 76

The U.S. Combined Joint Task Force 76 was working in Afghanistan during Operation Enduring Freedom in 2006. The task force report notes that the need for a KM initiative became clear when the commanding general made the following request: "I want to know how many missions over the last 30 days were conducted by the 3d Brigade Combat Team, and how many utilized aviation assets."

To answer that request, the task force staff had to search folders manually and make calls to subordinate units. It was a time-consuming process that resulted in a slow and inexact response. According to the report, that was no isolated incident.

The task force KM office examined the procedures used to coordinate information on missions and documented a number of problems, including the following:

▶ Each subordinate unit had different methods for tracking mission information such as that requested by the general, with a majority using static spreadsheets.

▶ When task force and subordinate staff sections were assigned a mission, each section planned the same mission in different ways.

▶ When preparing reports for general officers, operations personnel from different staff sections didn't have access to information from the other sections that was necessary to create a vision of the overall operation.

▶ There was no centralized repository for operations information. Much of the information existed only in individual email messages. For example, personnel in subordinate units attached electronic slide presentations to emails they sent to the chief of operations. These were then forwarded to personnel in appropriate staff sections and stored on individual computer stations.

▶ On average, supplying the information requested about mission status took 40 hours and involved manual searches by six subordinate units.

These examples demonstrated that the information-handling process was inefficient, cumbersome, and filled with opportunities for mistakes and breakdowns.

The solution that was developed reduced to 30 seconds the time required to locate the mission-specific information requested. (The specific design process used to create this KM system for the task force is described in more detail in chapter 6.) The solution included the following factors:

▶ A single format for entering report information. Using this reporting template to enter information directly into the database replaced the use of email messages to transmit data and produced information in standard report form.

▶ A centralized document library with controlled access where reports, presentations, and other task force information was posted.

▶ A database containing the most current information, accessible to the entire task force, to help the task force staff and subordinate staffs with a single access point for the latest mission and asset information.

It was clear that effective KM significantly improved task force operations. The new procedures and supporting software reduced search time to less than a minute and increased the information's accuracy.

The revised processes also

▶ opened a secure, real-time, collaborative information-sharing environment

▶ helped officers make critical decisions by providing relevant information available to the right person at the right time

▶ standardized an inconsistent and labor-intensive process

▶ gave the commanding general quick, relevant, and reliable answers

▶ developed a centralized, searchable database of past and ongoing task force operations.

The issues demonstrated by the task force's example are not unlike the challenges encountered in the business world. The need for coordination of efforts and information, the swift retrieval of vital data, the standardized format to make searches more efficient, and the ability to compare information to make quality decisions are needs shared by all organizations. And the elements that were incorporated into the task force's KM initiative are reflected in many of the most successful KM systems currently in use.

Common Elements of Successful KM Systems

Knowledge management systems that consistently yield the most effective results for their organizations typically have the following factors in common:

▶ The systems incorporate both documented knowledge and the wisdom that is housed exclusively in the minds and practices of experienced employees, presented in formats that match user preferences. These formats range from paper-based file-and-folder setups to combinations of sophisticated software, and they often are built on existing structures, such as additions to the company's current intranet.

▶ The systems include step-by-step procedures for compiling, confirming, circulating, and updating organizational knowledge.

▶ Job descriptions are created for every member of the KM system development team to ensure that there is accountability for work done at each of the five stages of the KM development initiative.

▶ Where applicable, technology such as specialized software, electronic communication systems, and use of the organization's intranet makes the accumulated and archived knowledge available to those who need it in distant locations. (Although high-tech tools are not prerequisites for creating a useful KM system, most organizations that have multiple locations find such tools to be necessary components.)

▶ To capture the knowledge and expertise of retiring employees, organizations use formal documentation, video and audio recordings, one-on-one interviews, and succession-focused mentoring.

▶ The systems establish "gathering places" such as online communities of practice or collaborative workspaces where current employees can share knowledge and discuss ongoing projects.

▶ The organizations work toward creating cultures of knowledge sharing through various incentives, such as rewarding contributions to the knowledge base, spotlighting executive personnel's use of the knowledge base, and recognizing innovations developed from information gathered through the KM system.

▶ The systems are updated continually and are revised and upgraded to answer new challenges that occur within the organization.

Basic Rule 2

Knowledge management systems must engage every department in the organization.

Organizationwide Support for Your KM System

Knowledge management is not solely the responsibility of an organization's information technology, human resources, or training departments. To be effective, a KM system should be organizationwide, both in its contributors and in its users. When the system is in its early development phase, engaging broad support may be a challenge because of organization members' natural resistance to new directions and initiatives.

This resistance may stem from fear of not being able to understand and use this new KM system. It may be connected to the idea that documenting the knowledge they have in their heads will replace the need to keep them in the organization. It's also a step out of the comfort zones that they've been operating in, even if that comfort zone was inefficient and outdated. And, ultimately, employees may not see the need for a KM system because they simply can't visualize the potential benefits for them.

The following activities are good ways to overcome some of that resistance and promote your KM system throughout an entire organization:

- ▶ Encourage executive support for the KM initiative by developing a well-defined project plan that includes a detailed timeline, documented project roles and authority levels, resource requirements, accountability and evaluation methods, risk mitigation and management plans, a training plan, and an ongoing communications strategy.
- ▶ Publicize the support of executive-level managers through organization communications and reveal the degree of their support by highlighting their allocation of time and resources.
- ▶ Be selective in your use of the term *knowledge management*. The term itself can cause confusion and link your effort to the failures that may have happened in earlier KM efforts. Instead, create your program as an answer to a current challenge, linking it directly to organizational goals to counter potential resistance and gain acceptance.
- ▶ Create a steering committee with representatives from across the organization. An effective KM system ultimately must address the needs of all departments, even if it begins with a focus in a limited area.
- ▶ If the system will include a customer service component, get input from current customers.

▶ Request input from the information technology department early in the process. At some point, the KM system will require computer-based tools and access to make it grow. Planning with that growth in mind ensures that the selected input and user formats will make the eventual transition seamless.

▶ Start small and expand incrementally. Introducing your KM program on too broad a basis will make inevitable small missteps at rollout appear disastrous.

▶ Begin in an area where quick wins are possible—for example, put a troubleshooting guide online for one of the most common equipment or process problems in the company. This is the type of victory that affects the bottom line directly and thus gains favorable attention from management and from employees looking for ways to contribute to the organization's success. Promoting these victories will build enthusiasm for the KM system as a whole.

Think About This

Don't underestimate the importance of small initial projects to draw attention to your knowledge management initiative. These can be more than just quick victories; they can serve as illustrations of KM to those who don't fully understand the concept and examples of what KM can accomplish for those who aren't yet convinced of its merit.

▶ At the earliest opportunity, post questions needing answers that will help you discover subject matter experts who may have been missed when the development team first identified the existing and valuable knowledge to be gathered and made accessible to the organization. The broader and deeper the knowledge base, the more productive the KM system.

▶ Recruit a group of key employees to serve as champions and spokespersons for the KM initiative. They can help other employees understand the benefits of the KM system and help dispel misconceptions about it. Target those employees who are influential and respected in the organization to spread the word and to help you discover any areas of concern among employees.

▶ Seek voluntary participation instead of mandating that employees put information into the system and use it for their research.

▶ Create communications that illustrate the benefits of using the system effectively. Give examples of how to use it in the day-to-day operations of a range of units and departments: highlight some of the most frequently searched topics, share positive anecdotes from people who've used the knowledge base successfully, and profile the experience of an employee who used the information from the knowledge base in the innovation of a new idea.

▶ Present training sessions to introduce employees to the methods of accessing and contributing to the KM system. These may be classroom training sessions that involve actual hands-on practice with searching the knowledge base. They may include meetings where supporting documentation is distributed with step-by-step instructions and where employees are invited to comment on both the format and the knowledge housed in the KM system.

▶ Use recognition and reward to spotlight subject matter experts for their vital contributions to the success of the system. Mention them in organization communications, create an award for outstanding contributions that influence organizational operations, or even present such tangible rewards as prizes or bonuses.

▶ Recognize and reward both employees who put valuable information into the system and employees who use the knowledge base in an outstanding manner. Publicize their contributions to the organization.

▶ Demonstrate the system's value by publicizing successes at each stage of the development process to build support for the future stages of the program. Continue to remind employees that this valuable resource exists and is being improved and updated continually.

Getting It Done

Think about and answer these questions:

1. Who are potential champions for knowledge management in your organization?
2. What departments should be represented on the KM steering committee?
3. What knowledge does this system need to provide to members of the organization?
4. Who are some of the subject matter experts in the organization?
5. What goals will the successful implementation of this program accomplish?

3

Determining Your Organization's KM Goals and Needs

 What's Inside This Chapter

In this chapter, you'll learn

▶ How to define the goals of your knowledge management system
▶ How to discover your organization's knowledge problems and needs
▶ How to focus your knowledge-sharing efforts through a knowledge audit.

Determining organizational needs and developing specific measurable benefits from an increased sharing of information should be the initial focus of an organization's knowledge management design team. The essential first step in developing a KM system is defining goals—what the system is expected to accomplish. Simply amassing large amounts of information is not the goal. Accumulating strategic and useful knowledge and creating a way to search and find relevant information quickly is the foundation of effective KM.

Most organizations are interested in improving one or more of the following factors: growth, innovation, productivity, and cost reduction (figure 3-1). In pursuit of those factors, all KM systems share many of the same basic goals: They strive to make successes repeatable and to recognize and avoid errors in the future. A successful system will shorten the learning curve for new employees and enable all members of the organization to participate in its growth by sharing the knowledge base efficiently. Even more important, a knowledge management system will help leaders make

Figure 3-1. What Can KM Do for Us?

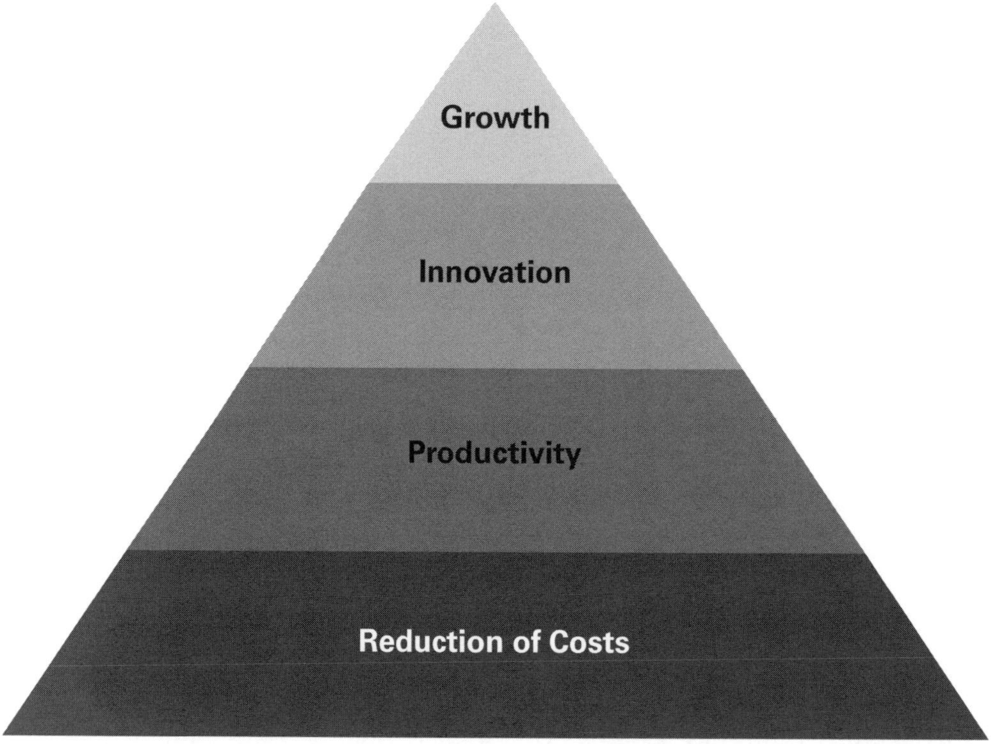

Growth

Innovation

Productivity

Reduction of Costs

more intelligent decisions based on both a complete understanding of past choices and a real-time menu of choices available currently.

Remember that every organization identifies different specific goals, depending on the nature of its business. For example, a service organization might have information needs based on frequently asked questions or on the rapid resolution of members' problems. A manufacturing plant's KM requirements might focus on product troubleshooting and maintenance issues or on completing product repairs swiftly. A retail business might want to develop an Internet site that gives customers direct access to product information and to brick-and-mortar store locations. Goals differ by organization, and those goals define each organization's KM needs.

It's vital to create goals for the KM system that mirror the business goals of the organization and to ensure that they include the concepts of SMART goals—Specific, Measurable, Achievable, Relevant, and Time-bound. Unless tangible results are achieved to answer specific organizational goals, management support for the KM system may not be sustained.

Basic Rule 3

An organization first should conduct a needs assessment to determine the goals, scope, and requirements of any knowledge management activities it is considering.

Identify What Knowledge Problems Must Be Corrected to Reach Those Goals

When goals and the knowledge to support them have been identified, it's time to define the organization's specific knowledge needs. As the development team begins to define those needs, it will discover many of the same issues that other organizations have faced when they began to create a KM system to serve their goals. Here are some questions about the existing state of knowledge in the organization. Answering these questions will help you and the development team identify specific problems that the KM system must address and may uncover some organizational information issues that have never before been evident:

▶ *Is the same process done differently in different areas of the organization?* Not all processes need to be regulated, but it's rare that an organization can't benefit immediately from some standardizing of processes.

▶ *Is there little or no coordination between similar information sources?* Improving communication systems is a major factor in reducing the duplication of efforts and in streamlining processes.

▶ *Are there multiple locations where the same information might be posted?* When this is the case, organizations profit not only from synchronizing information to make it easier to search and update, but also from reducing duplicate files on their servers and freeing up valuable space.

▶ *Are subject matter experts reluctant to share information for fear that it might be incorrect or incomplete?* Some organizations have discovered that an element of trust is lacking and needs to be added as they develop their systems. Where this is the case, ensuring a safe and collaborative atmosphere is a consideration in the early stages of the KM process.

▶ *Do subject matter experts understand what kinds of information could be useful to others?* The learning professional's role in helping

Noted

If HP knew what HP knows, we would be three times as profitable.
– Lewis E. Platt, CEO of Hewlett-Packard, 1992–1999

develop the KM system includes responsibility for enlightening resident experts on the varieties of knowledge that are beneficial to share.

▶ *Is there a fear of online technology that affects the sharing of information electronically?* Organizations that historically have been less dependent on technological systems have experienced the best results when they considered alternatives to a full-scale software implementation of their KM systems. The focus of the system is its content, and the system's success requires putting that content in a format that actually will be used.

▶ *When information is posted in a location for employees to access, is there little or no updating?* This can be discovered easily enough by looking at any posted policies and procedures. Are any of them outdated? The maintenance of these types of information can be a valuable goal for any KM program because it can reduce the risk of liability and dangerous misinformation.

▶ *Is there duplication of efforts because information is not shared?* Although processes are done differently in many departments, organizations consistently have found that the parallel efforts in different departments share similar characteristics. Sharing information on current processes and projects among departments and teams saves money, time, and resources.

▶ *Is there little recognition and use of any existing information systems? Is the current intranet rarely accessed?* Have existing resources become outdated without anyone noticing? If so, your new KM system will benefit from being clearly distinguished from the old system. Make certain the new system has both updated information and a visibly different format.

▶ *Is there currently no single location to find company information, policies, and procedures?* To see if this is a problem in your organization, look for various resources—company phone directories, HR documents, operating manuals, product information, policy and procedure manuals, employee handbooks, and current document templates. The length of time and the number of different locations that a person must visit to find any of these will indicate whether the KM system has to make centralizing needed data a priority.

▶ *Are there marketplace issues that need to be addressed by the KM system?* Consider present industry trends, the organization's competitive strategy, and new challenges in the niche.

By recognizing these issues, you and the KM system development team will begin to identify what the system needs to achieve its goals.

Think About This

It's important that those conducting the knowledge audit of your organization take time to perform in-depth analysis to ensure that their results reflect the actual knowledge problems, not just the symptoms of bigger issues.

Gather Input from Prospective Users: Make a Knowledge Audit

It's important to know what the organization needs from its KM system and equally important to know what those who will use the system need from it. Taking the time to poll employees on their issues and needs will focus your organization's KM system development efforts. A current *knowledge audit* identifies what knowledge the organization's employees (and where appropriate, its external customers) need, where and with whom that knowledge resides, and how that knowledge is accessed before the system is designed and implemented. Surveys, questionnaires, and face-to-face discussion sessions will bring the team closer to discovering what the system must provide.

The first layer of your knowledge audit will begin with written questionnaires and surveys completed by as many employees as possible. The subsequent analysis of the answers will help determine the areas for improved knowledge flow in your company. (It also may reveal some actions that will enhance your knowledge-sharing environment immediately—while the full-scale KM system is being designed and launched. We'll talk about that a little later in this chapter.)

Here are some sample survey items you can include in your initial KM questionnaire. Ask participants to rate their agreement with the statements, using the following five-point scale: 1 = completely agree, 2 = agree somewhat, 3 = have no opinion, 4 = disagree somewhat, 5 = completely disagree.

- People in our organization can identify the subject matter experts for departments, projects, products, processes, and equipment.
- Employees are able to access needed documents and processes easily.
- Policies are enforced consistently and are readily accessible and understood.
- Key information is accessible—readily and easily—to everyone who needs it.
- There is no conflicting information available to employees.
- It is easy to determine which version of a document is the most up to date.
- It is quicker to find information, documents, or projects than to recreate them.
- When an employee leaves the organization, the time it takes for others in his or her department to return to fully productive operations is minimal.
- Customers are able to find answers to the most frequently asked questions quickly and easily.
- Customer satisfaction scores are high for service and customer relations issues.
- Departmental activities proceed without interruption when key people are not immediately available.
- We reward individuals for sharing knowledge in our organization.
- Department members regularly document useful information and share it with others.
- We are working to capture the knowledge of retirees before they leave.
- There is little or no duplication of efforts across our organization.

As they are turned in, the questionnaires should be grouped by department, team, or functional unit. As you tabulate the results of each department's questionnaires, you'll find that the higher the scores, the more immediate the needs in that specific department. Additional analysis can be made by reviewing the ratings for each separate question to determine critical issues across multiple departments or units.

In the next phase of the knowledge audit, you'll perform face-to-face interviews, preferably with some of the people who completed the first questionnaire. You also can use informal conversations, group brainstorming sessions, and telephone and video conferences. Recognizing your organizational culture and the level of trust will help you choose the optimal formats.

For this layer of interviews, you'll want to include more in-depth questions. Here are some examples:

- ▶ What is your role in the organization and what does an average day include?
- ▶ What kinds of information do you need to do your job well?
- ▶ Where do you look for this information or whom do you have to ask?
- ▶ For what kinds of information are you most frequently asked?
- ▶ What challenges have you experienced in trying to find the information you need?
- ▶ What company resources (manuals, classes, checklists) have you found useful in gathering information?
- ▶ Do you use the company intranet to help with your day-to-day work?
- ▶ What sections of the intranet do you use most frequently?
- ▶ What kinds of information do you look for on the intranet? Can you give examples?
- ▶ What could make those searches easier for you?
- ▶ What are the first things new employees in your department need to learn to be able to do their jobs?

Through this interview and conversation process, you'll begin to identify areas of knowledge management that need attention. It's important to realize that not all of the findings of the knowledge audit will be welcome information. There may be some hard truths that have to be faced to move forward in this process. But not knowing those truths doesn't lessen their effect on the organization. Identifying and addressing them in your KM efforts will keep your organization from compounding past errors and will offer the opportunity to move forward.

At this point, you have two options. One option is to continue forward and conduct the final phase of your knowledge audit by identifying and locating the organization's current knowledge sources. The second option is to pick an area of the business that clearly will be helped by a KM process and implement a preview project focusing on that area's specific issue.

If you want to take the first option and complete the knowledge audit, skip the next section and go to "Getting It Done" at the end of the chapter. The rest of the audit is discussed in chapter 4. If there is an apparent need that can be answered right now by a focused KM effort, and the KM team chooses to take that detour, the next section will guide the process.

Creating a KM Preview Project

The detour to create a KM preview project is worthwhile if there is a demonstrated need. If not, it's best to continue through the full process.

Specific situations that may necessitate a preview project include the discovery of an urgent business need or a mission that's time sensitive; an easy-to-implement solution that will generate support from stakeholders, knowledge holders, or end users; or requested assistance for a group that is highly respected in the organization.

In deciding on a preview project, a good option is one that addresses a small group of employees so that you can keep the scope of the project manageable.

It's also beneficial if this project is in a department with a manager and employees who are more adaptable and open to change and where your project will produce measurable results. Perhaps it's the company call center where additional knowledge sharing could lead to immediately increased customer satisfaction. Incorporating the project with a customer satisfaction survey can exhibit the benefits of your knowledge management system more quickly than a process that solely affects the internal workings of a department.

Another preview project could be in your customer service department where each representative is answering the same customer questions with a different response. If a list of frequently asked questions with the correct answers is created, immediate benefits will be seen through reduced research time and increased consistency in service. This will translate into enhanced customer confidence and satisfaction.

A preview project that can affect the entire organization is identifying and collecting the current templates for all business documents, including press releases, form letters, PowerPoint presentations, memos, fax cover pages, reports, and other essential documents. The immediate benefits include a reduction in time spent recreating these documents, reduced opportunity for errors, and the presentation of a consistent brand image.

Think About This

A knowledge audit can be a time-consuming component of a KM initiative, but the results are worth the effort. The study of what knowledge is needed by employees, where that knowledge resides, and how it's currently accessed will allow the team to design the new KM system with a combination of what works now and what's needed.

Getting It Done

Think about and answer these questions:

1. What are the organization's goals and objectives?
2. How can this KM system address those goals?
3. What are the biggest challenges in the current methods of storing knowledge?
4. What individuals could help me identify the areas that are most affected by knowledge loss?
5. What are some potential challenges that could be quick wins for a first KM project?

4

Locating Information Sources in Your Organization

What's Inside This Chapter

In this chapter, you'll learn

▶ The difference between explicit and tacit knowledge
▶ How to locate knowledge sources in your organization
▶ How to find your company's subject matter experts
▶ How to cultivate a knowledge-sharing culture through recognition and reward.

To this point, your KM system development team has taken time to uncover the areas where your organization will benefit from knowledge management. Your next activities will take your knowledge audit through its final steps to document the sources of information that currently exist and to discover both resources and employees who are unappreciated holders of key organizational knowledge.

Basic Rule 4

Before creating knowledge management systems, the organization should identify existing formal and informal knowledge sources.

In this final phase of the knowledge audit, the team will be searching for the *core* knowledge that the organization needs to operate, the *advanced* knowledge that sets your organization apart from others, and the *innovative* knowledge that makes the organization unique.

What Knowledge Sources Already Exist?

Understanding the two main types of knowledge in your organization—explicit and tacit—will help you know where to look for each type.

Explicit knowledge is information that can be documented. Because it can be represented in text, figures, and symbols, it can be written and stored. You'll find explicit knowledge in product care-and-use manuals, how-to resources, process-flow documents, policies and procedures manuals, textbooks, and training class materials, as well as in documents posted at department communication centers, quick reference cards, and other tangible resources.

Tacit knowledge is more difficult to identify. It involves "know-how." It exists in the heads of employees, unwritten rules and processes, and problem-solving procedures. It includes networks, contacts, and relationships. Collecting tacit knowledge is time consuming, but if its collection and subsequent sharing are done with sensitivity and an honest appreciation of the people who hold this knowledge, it can yield a stronger knowledge base and can create a more collaborative work environment.

Discovering Explicit Knowledge Sources

Look for your organization's explicit knowledge in the following places:

▶ operating manuals for office and manufacturing equipment, process manuals, and catalogs and user manuals for products the organization makes

▶ employee handbooks, whether printed or prepared in any other format; these handbooks contain essential employee information, including dress codes, leave and vacation information, and conduct guidelines

▶ the organization's strategic plan, including the core values, mission statement, directors' minutes, and other guiding documents

▶ education and development tools, such as facilitator guides, background research, photographs, and illustrations

▶ training materials, including textbooks, class manuals, handouts, and learning aids

▶ audiovisual displays, including presentations to the board of directors, marketing materials, conference and tradeshow exhibits, and recruiting videos

▶ policies and procedures from HR, finance and accounting, and operations departments

▶ checklists for equipment, customer service processes, and safety practices

▶ lists of frequently asked questions for individual departments, new employees, and customers

▶ contents of department bulletin boards, including memos, letters, announcements, and safety notices

▶ memos, emails, letters, and other written missives stored in administrative files

▶ annual company reports and statistical information generated internally or externally

▶ directories of employees, networks, customers, competitors, and related industries (with contact information where suitable)

▶ calendars and event listings for company, community, professional, and trade organizations

▶ HR forms, including recruiting, hiring, performance management, and legal documents

▶ information technology forms, help desk records, and service requests

▶ accounting forms and policies, such as purchase orders, expense reports, and reporting instructions

- ▶ marketing materials, flyers, brochures, catalogs, advertisements, competitor profiles, and sales department research reports
- ▶ market and demographic reports on the community and the market that the organization serves
- ▶ vendor lists and ratings, price lists, recommendations, warnings, contact information, available discounts.

Many of these sources, which in the past might have been entirely paper documents, are now part of electronic networks, so locating the information will mean searching the company intranet, calendar and email software, list servers, databases, and other online information repositories.

Use the information generated in the second (interview) phase of the knowledge audit to identify the written and electronic files that employees use regularly. Searching and analyzing those files can help you find inconsistencies and duplicates and uncover information that other areas of the organization may need but don't know exists.

Gathering all of this explicit knowledge is an excellent beginning to a KM system because it enables your system development team to highlight those sources that already exist. Publishing a comprehensive list of these resources and their present locations gives you an instant win and engages new champions for the system as others recognize the value and uses of these information sources.

Discovering Tacit Knowledge Sources

Tacit knowledge includes the "who, what, why, when, where, and how" of everyday business—the organizational wisdom. This knowledge isn't discovered by looking up lists or reading documents. It's in the memories, experiences, and expertise of the organization's employees. It takes effort to compile this wisdom, but the results can be invaluable because this is the actual knowledge that is currently helping star employees succeed in the performance of their daily activities.

An excellent source of tacit knowledge exists in the daily activity and problem resolution practices of every team and department in the organization. For example, your call center and frontline employees are solving problems every day, and the resolution practices they use could be valuably applied throughout the organization. But if those practices aren't documented somehow, that tacit knowledge remains untapped.

Other sources that can be mined for tacit knowledge to compile into explicit sources include

- experiences of current, retiring, and past employees gathered in recorded oral histories, interviews, and written communications
- performance histories of initiatives and activities that have been tried and have succeeded—or failed
- employee comments, suggestions, notes from phone conferences, and meeting minutes
- notes from best-practices sessions and roundtable discussions
- notes of best practices recorded from discussions during informal training sessions, evaluations, and question-and-answer lists
- department meeting notes with action items and descriptions of projects that have been considered, tried, completed, or are in progress
- employees' verbal or written reports on projects and on conferences, tradeshows, and training sessions attended; their recommendations arising from the projects or events
- notes from strategic planning discussions, including background for decisions made, course corrections, and considerations

Noted

Some years ago, I gave a speech to a group of information, knowledge, and corporate communication executives. I was speaking about change, rather than knowledge management. But at the end I asked, "How many of you are comfortable sharing what you know?" Out of an audience of 200, only three hands went up. Clearly, if the people responsible for managing, creating, promoting, and leading the concept of sharing knowledge were uncomfortable doing it themselves, we were looking at a big problem—a human problem, not a technology problem.

– Carol Kinsey Goman, "Five Reasons People Don't Tell What They Know"

▶ notes from brainstorming sessions, including recommendations for action and ideas shelved for future consideration.

The challenge that tacit knowledge presents to the KM system development team is to design a system that can capture this type of information easily and quickly. If it's too difficult to put tacit information into the system, input will be slow, incomplete, or nonexistent. Additionally, if the people who have this knowledge are uncomfortable with submitting information that they don't feel is "perfect," they'll often avoid doing so.

Locating Subject Matter Experts in Your Organization

Organizations abound with subject matter experts, but many of them don't realize they are experts. Or they keep a low profile. Or they're afraid to attach the name "expert" to themselves for fear that others will scrutinize their activities and discover they're doing things incorrectly or that their managers will attach higher standards of performance to them.

Surveys and questionnaires will help, but most people resist proclaiming themselves experts on paper. So, although you'll want to use paper and on-line surveys and questionnaires for the ease that they bring to the process, you don't want to overlook the importance of face-to-face interviews as an effective way to identify and communicate with subject matter experts. These individual conversations help sustain the human touch that is needed to keep a knowledge management initiative from intimidating those it is meant to serve.

Here are some questions you can ask of employees to discover which of them have specific experience and expertise that will be worth gathering, archiving, and sharing through the KM system:

▶ *What sort of problems do you have to solve?* These might involve procedures and processes. They may be networking or organizational issues. Or they might be customer service challenges. You're looking for recurring challenges that could be addressed with better information up front.

▶ *Whom do you go to with questions on procedures?* This is your opportunity to begin locating subject matter experts you haven't identified yet. Is there a person who is more adept at people challenges, or someone who is the resident equipment expert? Is there a person who is the last word on office management questions or product information? These are potential sources of expert-level knowledge.

▶ *What questions do other employees frequently ask you?* This question can help you discover if the person you're interviewing is considered an expert by others in the department and what areas of expertise he or she brings to the knowledge base.

▶ *What questions do customers frequently ask you?* This question will assist not only in determining if a customer component is needed in your KM system, but also in developing a list of answers to frequently asked questions for employees who deal with the public or with external customers.

▶ *Whom do you go to with questions about technology problems?* This will be helpful to determine hardware and software experts both inside individual teams and departments and in your information technology unit.

▶ *Who is helpful in dealing with people and customer service issues?* These people are both potential experts and potential trainers, mentors, and facilitators for communities of practice in your organization.

▶ *Can you think of any customers who would be good candidates to survey on customer service needs?* If the development team has decided that a customer service component is needed in the KM system, this will help you gather a survey panel to ensure the system is useful and credible for customers.

Additionally, if the interviewee is receptive, you can include questions about her or his specific skills and abilities so you can identify additional areas that aren't part of her or his regular job duties but in which the person is accomplished and could be a subject matter expert. This is an opportunity to discover individual accomplishments that stretch beyond the boundaries of the workplace and might be valuable to the organization. You might be surprised to find a person who serves as an editor for a volunteer organization would be thrilled at the chance to write for your KM newsletter.

Remember that your discussions and interviews aren't only intended to learn what information you can get from the people you're questioning. They also should find out what information the interviewees need or want from others. By modeling this two-way use of knowledge, you begin to show that the system will include material that makes their daily tasks easier and more productive.

Encourage a Knowledge-Sharing Culture in the Organization

An organization will be most successful in its KM system efforts if it develops and supports a culture where sharing knowledge is valued and encouraged. Overcoming the hoarding of knowledge by people who fear they'll sacrifice job security if they let loose what they know is a key task in creating a climate that nurtures sharing. Recognizing and rewarding people who share their knowledge with coworkers and customers will ensure the continuation and expansion of the KM system.

Avoid the Knowledge-Hoarding Pitfalls

Two of the common mistakes made by the developers of KM systems are assuming (1) that employees always will share their knowledge on request and (2) that workplaces operate in a completely organized manner that can be identified and replicated easily.

There are myriad reasons why employees are reluctant to share their knowledge. They often don't realize the value of what they know, or they do know its value and are scared someone will misuse the information for their personal gain. And then there's that timeless issue of resistance to change. Many managers withhold information, doling it out like a miser only when it's desperately needed; or they ask for input when all they really want is someone to agree with them. With those experiences, it's not surprising when employees are hesitant to share their knowledge.

People may be resistant to a program that makes them share knowledge, thereby prompting them to feel dispensable and replaceable. Anger over evaluations or a lack of promotion, or worry that someone else will get credit for their knowledge also may inhibit their sharing.

Process and policy issues may be barriers to knowledge sharing. A lack of proper forums in which to share knowledge, no time to share, a lack of understanding about which knowledge is confidential, or even the idea that knowledge sharing is not part of their job description may keep employees from participating. And when knowledge sharing is not modeled by supervisors, managers, and executives, that resistance is intensified.

The KM system development team has to address these knowledge-capture issues before it considers system design and technology because knowledge is the central and critical element—the entire reason for making the effort. A culture of knowledge sharing must be cultivated along with a feeling of trust and confidence that shared information will be used wisely. That trust and confidence requires the support and action of the organization's leaders; they must model the behavior they want others to emulate. This is a key characteristic of knowledge-sharing environments.

To make your way around many of the knowledge-hoarding barriers, you need to know what motivates people to embrace the concept of knowledge sharing. Let's think about ourselves and some of the reasons we share knowledge with others. Our basic feeling is that we need to share what we know as part of our jobs. We like people and want to help them, we want to build on knowledge, and we enjoy being part of a community. Often we're seeking input and suggestions, and we realize that getting information requires giving information. We want to move upward in our careers or to learn about other areas of the organization. We're always looking for ways to do our jobs more easily or more effectively, and often we simply enjoy creating mutually beneficial relationships. We want our companies to succeed because we want to be part of a winning team. And, of course, recognition and reward can be strong motivators, as can the negative perception attached to those who are not forthcoming in sharing information.

Considering these motivators will help you incorporate the right mix of participation incentives in your KM system. Organization members need to understand that knowledge sharing not only benefits the group, but also helps them as individuals.

Create KM Reward and Recognition Practices

Because the adage "knowledge is power" fuels knowledge hoarding in most organizations, your KM system will benefit from incorporating recognition and reward features into your activities. The goal is to change "knowledge is power" to "knowledge is a dynamic asset that grows through sharing."

Traditionally, the business world has tended to recognize those people who *have* knowledge, rather than those who share it. Organizations value their "go-to" person or that person of whom everyone in a department is continually asking questions. This has encouraged people to focus on individual knowledge rather than on collective knowledge. To nurture an information-sharing organization, it's important to develop practices that recognize and reward people for contributing and sharing information rather than merely possessing it.

Here are some guidelines and concepts that you'll want to keep in mind when creating a recognition or reward program:

▶ *Recognition* is visible, public reinforcement to individuals and teams for contributing and for modeling desired behaviors; *rewards* are tangible items, such as money or gifts.

▶ Recognition or reward may be at the individual, team, community, group, department, business, or enterprise level. An individual's preferences should be considered in any recognition: some people are not comfortable with public praise and some thrive on it. Using managers' knowledge of their employees can help ensure that appropriate recognition methods are used.

▶ Recognition does not have to be accompanied by reward. A pat on the back, a mention in a meeting or newsletter, or a public announcement honors knowledge-sharing practices and encourages others by example.

▶ Rewards don't require ceremony. Many organizations privately present items of tangible value to discourage negative responses, such as jealousy or unfair comparisons by those who feel their contributions weren't as highly regarded.

▶ Rewards can be positive and excellent incentives, but they also can have a negative effect if there is any perception of unfairness or scarcity. And individual rewards may encourage competition instead of teamwork.

▶ Careful evaluation is necessary before implementing any reward or recognition system to determine factors such as the duration of the program. The challenge here is that if you connect rewards to behavioral changes, you may lose the activity when the rewards decline.

It should be noted that many effective recognition and reward practices aren't used to encourage people to start sharing their knowledge. Instead, they honor those people and groups who have made significant contributions to the organization's knowledge base, thus motivating others to do the same.

Best-practices organizations use a blend of different approaches to reinforce knowledge sharing. Some collect usage reports on their KM software systems so they can recognize their most active contributors and users and highlight successes. Other organizations host knowledge-sharing recognition events. Other organizations embed knowledge sharing as part of daily work routines and don't reward people directly for knowledge contributions. Instead, they rely on the link between knowledge sharing and work performance to reinforce the practice. In fact, an increasing number of these organizations incorporate contributions to the knowledge base as part of their performance appraisal criteria.

Recent studies have shown that organizations also get results from changing the focus of their reward programs. Instead of connecting rewards with contributions to the knowledge base, they reward the successful use of information that's in the database. In such cases, people are rewarded for getting projects completed ahead of time through effective use of the knowledge database, and they are encouraged to cite the database sources they used. Then those people who contributed that knowledge also are recognized or rewarded.

Perhaps the most effective method for getting employees involved as "knowledge workers" is direct communication—discussing knowledge sharing with members of the organization. Only when they truly understand the importance of this initiative, how it can help them, and how vital they are to the success of the effort will they begin to embrace the changes that you are asking them to make. If you want people to share what they know, you need to make it clear that the sharing is for a good reason and that the organization is willing to invest the resources and time needed to gather the knowledge and make it available to others who will use it in support of the organization's goals. And they need to see that the organization so values their willingness to share that it invests in recognizing and rewarding contributors. They need to see the big picture—what an improvement this can make in their daily operations. And often all of this is best communicated in person.

Getting It Done

Think about and answer these questions:

1. Using the lists from this chapter, what explicit knowledge sources can your team identify?
2. Using the lists from this chapter, what tacit knowledge sources can your team identify?
3. What additional questions can be used to interview the organization's subject matter experts?
4. What will be the contributions of a KM system to your organization's success?
5. What will be the benefits of a KM system for the members of your organization?

5

Creating Your KM Blueprint

What's Inside This Chapter

In this chapter, you'll learn

▶ How to gather and evaluate existing knowledge
▶ How to assess and implement tools to capture new knowledge as it is generated
▶ How to house this knowledge in a system that addresses your organizational needs and culture.

By this point, your KM team has made tangible progress. You've determined why the organization needs to manage its knowledge, and you've discovered what information is used in the organization and how it's shared. You've also identified existing information sources and have developed an understanding of some of the potential pitfalls typically encountered in putting a KM system together. Now it's time for the third step in the KM system design process: gathering existing knowledge and selecting and creating formats to capture knowledge going forward. This is where the main components of knowledge management—people, processes, and technology—come together to form knowledge bases.

Gather the Organization's Existing Knowledge

Your organization houses a wealth of knowledge. It's that knowledge that gives the organization its strategic advantage in the marketplace. The task ahead of your KM team now is to collect that knowledge from the places it resides so you can create a way to ensure that knowledge is available to others in the organization who need it to make informed decisions and plans.

Basic Rule 5

The design of a knowledge management system should be based on desired results *and* on the organization's culture and expertise.

Gathering explicit knowledge requires the study and analysis of existing documents, a review of how information flows in the organization, and analysis of written records (the records may be in any form, from manuals and textbooks to blogs, reports from the help desk, and meeting minutes). Gathering tacit knowledge includes a great deal of personal contact that requires excellent communication and active listening skills, competent interviewing techniques, and both research into and review of best practices and lessons learned.

Your KM officer will distribute the knowledge gathered to the team members, organizational authorities, and the newly identified subject matter experts for their review. They'll assess the existing knowledge by answering the following questions:

▶ Is the knowledge useful to a larger population of the organization?
▶ Is the knowledge complete and useful as it is?
▶ How does this knowledge fit in with the goals of the organization and the strategic knowledge management goals that were determined by the KM team?

▶ What will be the best format to house this knowledge?

▶ Is this knowledge complete as is, or will it continue to expand either occasionally or on a regular basis?

Your team will want to brainstorm and add any other questions that relate to your organization's specific needs from its KM system.

Choose Methods to Capture Knowledge Going Forward

The capture of future knowledge will be easier for the KM team because of the time and effort put into creating templates and multiple methods for members of the organization to input knowledge quickly and easily. Additionally, the time spent analyzing existing knowledge helps refine the standards and speed up decision making on whether submitted knowledge needs to be made a permanent part of the knowledge base.

Because the organization's intranet or extranet can host many of the different options listed in this section, it's important to have IT representatives involved early in the process to ensure that your KM team knows what is possible with your current technology and resources.

While we most often hear of software systems as the home for knowledge bases, this is only one of the many forms your KM system may take. Software or an intranet system may be your entire knowledge solution, or it may be part of a larger solution that includes various formats. Conversely, it may not be a part of the solution at all in the early stages of the knowledge management process.

A wide variety of knowledge initiatives can be adapted to address your issues and challenges in knowledge sharing. Among those are social and networking initiatives such as mentoring, leadership training, collaboration, recruitment, cross-training, and other education and development activities. They may focus on organization and technology systems, including records management, search-and-find features, innovation management, workplace design, online training, or training directed to mobile devices such as PDAs (personal digital assistants).

Building on these kinds of initiatives that already exist in your organization can result in some of the most effective blended formats for KM systems. They require less development time because they are already in place and

Think About This

KM is most effective when it includes an integration of various knowledge-sharing methods. Although technology systems are excellent in helping facilitate the capture and dissemination of knowledge, organizations with effective KM systems have noted that enabling connections among people is where they discover their greatest success stories.

they meet with reduced resistance because they are an accepted part of the organizational culture.

Let's review a selection of the processes and formats for capturing knowledge as it's being generated.

After-Action Reviews

An *after-action review* is a short, focused meeting, held after an event or project, in which the people who orchestrated or participated in the event or project discuss the goal, the actual result, the reasons for any discrepancies between those two elements, and what lessons were learned. People at the meeting share this information so the organization can continue building on these experiences.

Following some basic guidelines helps produce after-action reviews that result in the most complete evaluations of projects. For example, hold the meeting as soon as possible after the project or event ends to ensure that details are fresh and can be discussed more specifically than would be possible at a later date. Include all the key people involved, and invite customers if it's appropriate. Begin the meeting by recalling the event's or project's measurable goals and decide whether those goals were met. Do a step-by-step review of activities, and ask for comments on what went well and what could have gone better. This information should be documented by the facilitator and posted on an appropriate forum so that future similar activities can build on the successes and avoid the difficulties encountered.

If properly facilitated, after-action reviews can identify practices that will simplify future planning. If not structured with specific questions and effective control of the discussion, they can end up as free-form conversations with no lasting value.

Best-Practice Sessions

A *best-practice session* brings peers together to share prior work and experiences so that the knowledge gained can be used and expanded by others in their own work. These sessions can be facilitated by learning professionals with invitations to members of the organization who share similar job duties, management levels, or developmental interests. These meetings can be structured to include practices about a specific topic or general activities related to the participants' positions and responsibilities.

These sessions can be valuable opportunities to address specific problems and questions posed by those in attendance. The challenge is to avoid allowing them to turn into gripe sessions where attendees join in complaining about those problems. A strong facilitator can help avoid this possibility.

Communities of Practice

Communities of practice are networks that enable organizations to capture and build on the expertise of a group of individuals with similar areas of operation. These areas may be for individuals in the same positions, for specific job responsibilities, or based around events or professional interest areas such as marketing or training. These communities may exist in person, online, or as a combination of both; and they enable the members to develop an ongoing relationship that makes it possible and comfortable to discuss issues, seek assistance, or offer answers to questions asked of the group.

The KM officer can appoint a moderator or facilitator from among the community's subject matter experts to organize meetings of the community, maintain lists of email addresses and other contact information, monitor the network for standards of conduct, and serve as the group's contact point. This person can help enlist members and gain interest for the group by coming up with a few questions on specific issues relevant to the community and posting them online to initiate conversations.

If the group will meet only online or through some other mechanism that involves technology, the moderator needs to ensure that all members of the group are comfortable using that technology and will have to train members who don't possess those skills at an early stage.

If possible, it's best to give communities who ultimately will meet exclusively online an opportunity meet in person at least once. This helps the group members bond and build relationships. All communities have to determine the mission and goals of the community, set codes of conduct, and assign responsibilities. That work is more easily accomplished when there is some level of in-person interaction at the outset.

The moderator will want to create archives of important questions that are addressed by community members and the research and answers that resulted from those discussions. Additionally, he or she occasionally will want to poll the participants to ensure that they wish to remain members or to seek their recommendations for people to add to the group. Successful communities avoid having members who don't participate in discussions or activities.

And, as with all committees and task forces, the KM officer will want to regularly evaluate the group to establish whether the network is still useful or whether it's time for its work to be concluded.

Blogs

Shorten the term *weblog* and you get *blog,* a type of electronic communication that's widely used personally and commercially to express opinions and create journals. But blogs also may be used in the workplace to capture information. Specific communities of practice may use blogs as a "meeting space" by posting questions or ideas and allowing comments to be added. Or they may post meeting minutes and information on group activities in a blog. An advantage of this is that blog entries normally are archived for future reference in reverse chronological order, with the most recent updates at the top of the list.

Departments can appoint representatives to archive their knowledge base in a blog format by creating brief entries about individual topics, tagging them with key words to make searches easier, and posting them to the site. Additional features such as columns on recent developments, reports on current topics, and space for comments and questions are easily accommodated in blogs as well.

The organization can use a blog as its homepage and include news about the company, specific events, celebrations, important notices, and highlighted links to any knowledge bases that have had recent updates to their information. The page becomes an information center with the latest news for the organization while it retains the feel of a communication medium that's more relaxed and personal than a traditional organizational homepage.

Because blogs are organic and generally not tightly fettered by rules and expectations, they can capture an extensive range of information: photographs, audio or video presentations, calendars and schedules, polls, employees' accomplishments and recognitions, and links to external sites of interest and current news. For the same reasons, they can be difficult to monitor and regulate. Care must be taken to ensure that their informal nature doesn't give rise to conversations that are unprofessional or inappropriate.

Narrative Databases

A *narrative database* is essentially an oral history or commentary. It may be created by one person interviewing another, by one or more people gathering around a microphone and talking about what they know, or by recording presentations made by organization leaders. It can capture performance histories, participant comments, and anecdotes from the communities of practice where experience and tacit knowledge reside. It may comprise audio files, videos, or transcripts of discussions to ensure that the information is conveyed in a speaker's own words. Narrative databases can be especially useful in capturing the wisdom of retiring employees. These can become resources that are infrequently accessed unless they are edited into brief answers to specific questions or excerpted for use in company programs.

Online Training

As learning professionals and subject matter experts create new learning modules, information from these courses can be captured for inclusion in the knowledge base. The knowledge may be as simple as step-by-step instructions on how to operate equipment or how to complete a specific company report properly. Or it may be in areas of special interest, such as event planning or meeting management. These trainings can be accessed through the organization's learning management system, as entries on an intranet or extranet, or even through open source platforms that serve as gateways to training (like Moodle, at http://moodle.org).

Mobile Training

Also, as we're seeing in the latest developments, your organization can even access training on mobile devices such as cell phones, PDAs, and mp3 players. Consider being able to look up the latest information on your products and the market immediately before you walk into a customer's location and you can imagine how effective this use of knowledge management could be to your organization's bottom line.

Although these devices offer features for browsing and knowledge retrieval from the KM system, the recording capabilities and emailing features also qualify them as knowledge capture methods. Information may be recorded and immediately transmitted to KM monitors for consideration and validation. The value of these devices as KM tools is undetermined because they're so new as a form of knowledge capture.

Peer Assists

Peer assists are meetings of people from across the organization (or possibly from other organizations) who have some particular expertise and are asked to help a team on a specific project. They're convened by a team that needs assistance, and they enable participants to share best practices, insights, and ideas.

To be productive sessions, peer assists require strong facilitation and careful selection of invitees.

Wikis

A *wiki* is an online platform that allows users to quickly add and edit information to listings. An excellent example is the online encyclopedia, Wikipedia, where visitors are invited to update listings on topics in which they have expertise.

Wikis let users add information directly into the knowledge base, allowing the listings to include input and viewpoints from a number of different sources. An organization may host a variety of wikis, including topic-based, departmental, or troubleshooting forums.

Best-practice organizations using wikis have reduced email time because online editing eliminated back-and-forth emails to reach consensus. They've also expanded opportunities for collaboration, improved employee engagement in the creation of knowledge, and created an expanded knowledge base for market intelligence data.

To ensure that wikis start out right, the KM team should create a simple set of instructions for posting to the wiki and should display a few sample entries. Establish a set of guidelines for use of the wiki and create a code of conduct and policies defining the type of information that can be posted there.

The KM officer will appoint as wiki moderator an employee with excellent communication capabilities, coaching skills, and knowledge of the organization. This person's main role is to encourage discussion, request confirmation of information, and monitor entries for appropriateness. The moderator will remind users to include key words or identifying phrases, also known as *tags,* so people searching the wiki can do it effectively and quickly.

The KM team will want to ensure that they have developed a wiki layout that is user friendly and uncluttered to attract employees to use the site. A clear catalogue of entries should be included to encourage browsing so that visitors will have an opportunity to learn about areas of interest they hadn't considered when they decided to visit the wiki. If it's a public wiki, the team also will want to ensure that sensitive or proprietary information doesn't find its way onto the site.

Yellow Pages

An excellent way to discover and capture the knowledge possessed by individuals in your organization is to create a *"yellow pages"* system. For this

Think About This

If an organization's traditional intranet is stale and doesn't attract visitors anymore, a wiki is one option that can encourage active participation. The frequent updates and employee-focused information of wikis, blogs, and other interactive tools can help create new interest in the site.

employee-operated resource, a template is created by the KM team to make it easy for employees to list specific processes in which they are proficient (figure 5-1). By creating these reference pages, employees help others in the organization search for experts in areas where they need assistance or

Figure 5-1. What Can KM Do for Us?

ABC Services

A to Z | Site Map | FAQs | Search [＿＿＿＿＿＿] GO

About Us

Calendar

News

Staff Directory

Departments

Publications

FAQ

**ABC Services
1000 Main Street
Alexandria, LA 71348**

318.555.1234

STAFF DIRECTORY: Employee Profiles

David Woods

Position: Training Director
Email: DWoods@ABCSvcs.com
Phone: 318.555.1239
Location: Alexandria Home Office
Department: Education and Development

Conducts and supervises training and development programs for employees

Current committees include
KM Project Management Team (Chair)
Strategic Planning Team 2010

Communities of Practice:
Facilitator Forum
Mobile Tech

Certifications, Knowledge, Skills, and Abilities:
Master Facilitator
Project Management Certification
Certified Speaking Professional
Behavioral Interviewing Certification
Communications, Management, Leadership, Customer Service

Past Projects and Experience:
Information Servcies, Radio and Television Production, Conference Planning, Association Management

Languages:
English, Spanish, Russian

Joined ABC Services:
February 15, 2005

Related Press Releases:
15 February 2005 DWoodsTrainingDirector
3 June 2007 DWoodsAward

specific items of knowledge.

Creating a format that includes space for information about specific projects on which the experts have worked gives listees a way to describe their areas of expertise. Adding places to note specific skills, interests, and even skills they would like to develop can take this directory even further into an opportunity for cross-training and mentoring.

Employees can personalize the directory, if desired, by including photos, favorite quotes, or other material that expresses their individuality or personality. The danger of personalizing the directory inappropriately can be avoided by creating a template to keep a level of professionalism.

Noted

Business is a conversation because the defining work of business is conversation—literally. And "knowledge workers" are simply those people whose job consists of having interesting conversations.
– David Weinberger, *The Cluetrain Manifesto: The End of Business as Usual*

Designing the KM System

At this point, your KM team will determine which systems the organization currently uses and which ones to add to the knowledge management system. It will want to consider the organization's comfort level with technology and software applications to determine which of these solutions would be appropriate. The team also will want to look at the number of locations in which the organization operates or has offices. If the organization is spread across multiple sites, it will probably require online solutions to offer immediate access to information sources for individuals in distant locations.

The team will evaluate and select the formats you'll use to begin KM efforts from the list of information sources identified in this chapter and additional research through communities of practice, associations, and networking.

Think About This

By using a combination of features ranging from personal networking to document management and software search features, an organization can tailor a KM system to meet its organizational goals and business needs, while still addressing the preferences of its workforce.

Regardless of the design of the organization's KM system, it will need to include a *portal*—a gateway to the knowledge base that allows access and browsing of information, as well as virtual team collaboration and management of knowledge. The advantage of having this gateway is that the single point of entry ensures that the user is accessing all the latest information on a given topic.

Specialized KM software offers a multitude of options in collaboration, e-learning components, and the cataloguing of knowledge for organizations. Many of these incorporate a variety of the different formats listed here, such as bulletin boards, blogs, wikis, forums, networks, and even chat rooms where real-time discussions can be held online.

Software solutions often allow collaborative workspaces and the housing of documents for virtual teams. These teams incorporate all the principles of standard project management, use technology to bridge the space among members, and allow ongoing communication when face-to-face meetings are not an option.

Dedicated software can offer ideal solutions for KM needs, and extensive research should be done in advance to determine your organization's requirements, proficiency in the use of technology and software systems, and the software options that are currently available before selecting a vendor or package.

Although technology usually receives the most money and attention, the "bells and whistles" aren't what create a successful system. Technology is important because it enables KM system creators and users to incorporate knowledge management practices into their regular work operations. Ultimately, however, a KM system is only as good as the data it contains—a level of value directly dependent on the comprehensiveness of the data in the system and the care and accuracy of the people who gathered and entered that data. Remember the familiar maxim: junk in, junk out. Without committed people fully participating in the creation of the KM system, even the most expensive and user-friendly technology won't yield good results.

It's excellent if your system enables the KM team and organization leaders to track how often visits to the knowledge base result in an answer to the problem or yield the needed information. This could be done by allowing employees to rate the information they access with a numerical rating system or by posting online surveys with a simple query like "Did this article answer your question?"

Additionally, it's excellent if your software solution includes a dashboard—a tracking mechanism that displays the number of visits to the knowledge base, the average time spent, and other statistics that will enable the project team and senior managers to evaluate the usage of the knowledge initiatives.

It's also important for the system to establish a specific area of the database where members of the organization can post descriptions of any difficulties they experienced using the system so the KM team can get immediate feedback. Having links and email addresses to communicate problems, compliments, or concerns is also important to develop the users' loyalty to the system.

Ultimately, the KM system your team designs should include the ability to capture existing knowledge and incorporate new knowledge—often called "collect and connect." Whether the final system encompasses software solutions or is powered by people with paper, the key is to create the single gateway that leads people to the latest knowledge of the organization. And whether online or in person, the monitors and subject matter experts in the networks must be the guardians of the knowledge, and they are responsible for ensuring the accuracy of its content.

Getting It Done

Think about and answer these questions:

1. What are the questions your KM team will ask to assess the value of existing knowledge?

2. Which of the methods of capture for new knowledge seem best suited to the organization?

3. What additional research will your KM team do before designing the KM system for the organization?

4. What features are mandatory for your KM system?

5. In what system options has your KM team expressed an interest?

6

Compiling, Confirming, and Circulating the Knowledge

What's Inside This Chapter

In this chapter, you'll learn

- ▶ How to compile the information from knowledge sources
- ▶ How to create standards to verify and confirm the validity of the knowledge gathered
- ▶ How to open your knowledge management system to traffic.

From all the scattered sources and various versions of documents that the KM system development team has reviewed so far, it's obvious that submissions to the knowledge base need to be monitored continually and updated regularly to ensure that they're useful to members of the organization. To keep knowledge assets current, existing information will be reviewed at established intervals and new information will be confirmed before it's made available for circulation. Compiling the organization's knowledge, confirming its accuracy and currency, and circulating it throughout the organization are the tasks at hand.

Compiling the Organization's New Knowledge

In many of the formats discussed in chapter 5—online communities, wikis, blogs, and other electronic media—the owners of the knowledge put the information directly into the system. That leaves the system monitors primarily responsible for sending the information to the subject matter experts for approval or revision.

Considerations at this point can focus on increasing the ease of submitting knowledge to the KM system. As the system becomes more widely used, the KM team and users will discover other template ideas and standards that will further refine the KM system.

In creating templates for inputting knowledge, it's helpful to the system contributors and monitors if those templates are easily recognized through a consistent look and placement of recurring information so needed material can be identified, input, and verified quickly. For example, here are some questions that can be part of any template that addresses problem resolution:

- ▶ What problem occurred?
- ▶ What were any specific issues related to this problem?
- ▶ What were key statements that seemed to help stabilize the situation while you sought a resolution?
- ▶ Who was a resource for you in resolving this situation?
- ▶ Where did you find the information you needed to solve the problem?
- ▶ What did you do?
- ▶ What was the outcome?
- ▶ What follow-up will you do?
- ▶ What would you suggest that others do differently if this situation happens to them?

Remind all users and monitors that no sensitive information may be included in public listings.

For electronic listings, the template should require the user to add key words into the document description so that searches will be able to locate relevant information more easily.

Think About This

Remember the KM experience described in chapter 2—the example of the U.S. Army's Combined Joint Task Force 76? Battlefield strategists needed rapid and precise data, so the KM officer designed a system that consolidated up-to-date information and made it swiftly searchable. Here is the task list that helped to design and implement that system:

► Identify essential sources of the knowledge needed (including sources located outside the unit); decide when the knowledge was needed, how it should be formatted, and how it must be made available if the unit is to accomplish its mission.

► Develop a taxonomy or system of organization for storing and managing content of the KM system.

► Decide where and how content will be created, organized, applied, and shared in the system.

► Standardize content as much as possible. Use templates to ensure all data is entered properly.

► Develop a process for organizing knowledge so it can be discovered and managed throughout its life cycle. This process should add identifying features within the content to help users discover and retrieve the specific information they need and enable managers to track it.

► Decide who will manage the documents.

► Identify the technology available for managing content.

► Develop templates for storing and presenting documents.

► Establish content management processes for internal management.

► Decide if identifying and managing documents will be done at the unit level or at the organization level.

► Identify roles and set content access rights.

► Design the work flow for updating and revising content.

► Decide if documents are needed by a larger audience.

► Send appropriate documents for conversion to other hypertext markup languages to support wider dissemination.

► Tag documents with key words to facilitate more effective search and retrieval.

► Establish the period of time for which each document will be considered valid.

► Confirm with the operations security officer the control measures for physical security, operations security, classified documents, and dissemination.

For your template, choose a few questions that are relevant for your organization or let people select from a list of questions those that best suit
their situations. Remember that the easier it is to input information, the more
likely the survey will receive responses. If the survey is too lengthy, people
will delay putting the information in, memories and details will fade, and
chances are great that they won't submit any input at all.

Compiling the Organization's Existing Knowledge

For information that exists in hard-copy, audiovisual, or other nonelectronic
formats, the monitor's job is a little more complex. That data may have to be
transferred to some electronic format to make it accessible to the system. The
KM team will use considerations such as business goals, the number of people
to whom each document will be useful, and the length of time the information
in the document will continue to be current to determine which documents
merit electronic conversion and what resources are better left in their current
locations and formats, with notes or indexes that direct users to them.

Remember that the knowledge gathered and captured may need to take
a number of different forms, based on the various prospective users in your
organization (see figure 6-1). For example, step-by-step troubleshooting
guidance that's appropriate for your frontline employees and customer service call center is not the same information that will be useful for your techni-
cians. It may be that the information being compiled ends up in a number of
different formats, of varying lengths, and in differing degrees of complexity
to suit the multiple levels of proficiency in your organization.

To collect relevant knowledge into the KM system on a continuing basis,
the KM project team will have to review the organization's identified needs
and decide if the knowledge gathered and submitted addresses and satisfies
those needs. By reviewing knowledge assets with the departments involved
and with subject matter experts for those topic areas, the development team
can determine what information gathered from one department is relevant
for other areas of the organization.

The KM officer and team must define and communicate the desired level
of input quality in clear and specific terms to enable contributors to know
what is expected of them. After establishing the quality standards, the team
should create sample knowledge base entries as illustrations.

Figure 6-1. Questions to Ask When Compiling Knowledge

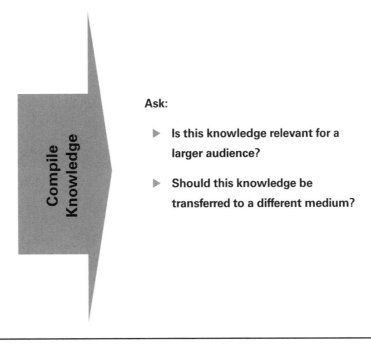

Compile Knowledge

Ask:

▶ **Is this knowledge relevant for a larger audience?**

▶ **Should this knowledge be transferred to a different medium?**

Validating and Verifying Knowledge Before Adding It to the KM System

When it has been determined that the knowledge is valuable to others, the KM team or the monitors assigned to that section will forward the information to the experts in that topic area for validation through confirmation of the information, updates, and any revisions or additions needed.

Validating and updating information continually ensures a high-quality knowledge database. If these processes are neglected, errors and inconsistencies will reduce users' confidence in the system and seriously decrease its utility and value.

The defined standards of quality and the established templates to input knowledge make it easier for the people in charge of verifying the information to measure the input against the intended end product. In addition to the accuracy, completeness, and timeliness of the knowledge put into the system, the people designated to validate it must ensure that all documents in the

Basic Rule 6

Effective KM systems enable the organization to share its knowledge *and* discover inconsistencies in its knowledge.

knowledge base are in a universally accessible software program available to all members of the organization. If the entry is in a blog, wiki, or other online resource, monitors should make sure that it includes a contact point or link to the subject matter expert. Because the alphabet soup that's produced when people make extensive use of acronyms is certain to confuse readers, content monitors must ensure that all acronyms used in entries are defined in a list or at their first use in any article or submission.

When knowledge has been gathered and compiled, it should be circulated to subject matter experts and communities of practice monitors who will review the information, ask questions, make corrections, and add any comments they might have (figure 6-2). *One caveat:* This is the point where KM teams may discover that even subject matter experts disagree about some information held or processes being used in the organization. When this situation occurs, team members responsible for validating information in that topic area will need to detour and solicit input from higher-level authorities for the final word on what is correct. Each time this happens, the KM process will slow down. But don't despair. This is knowledge management *in action* because information is being expanded and enhanced.

Finally, when it's been added to and amended by the appropriate experts and communities of practice, the information is ready for final posting to the knowledge base.

Circulating the Information in the KM System

At this point, it's time to post the verified and validated information to the knowledge management system the team has set up (figure 6-3) and to begin the pilot-testing phase. Starting with a limited number of users will give the KM team a chance to identify and make needed adjustments before opening the system to the entire organization.

Figure 6-2. Questions to Ask When Confirming Knowledge

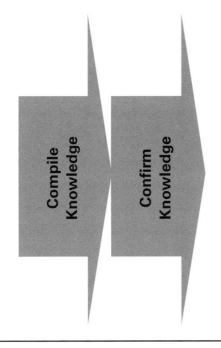

Ask:

▶ **Who are the subject matter experts on this knowledge?**

▶ **Is this knowledge correct, complete, and up to date?**

▶ **What format or template should this knowledge use?**

This is another point in the process of KM development where the experience and expertise of learning professionals is invaluable. These professionals will be responsible for designing and presenting meetings and workshops to teach users how to access and post information and to reinforce the standards of quality for postings. Initial sessions will include the pilot group who will not only be able to use the information in the limited rollout, but also will be able to evaluate and make recommendations on the content and delivery of the training sessions.

Rolling Out the KM System

To ensure orderly progress through the next steps of unveiling the KM system, your team will want to use a detailed project plan with deadlines based on the size of the organization and the scope of the initial knowledge base.

Here are steps to include in the KM rollout:

▶ The KM team determines the date for the organizationwide rollout. This will depend on the changes that need to be made from the pilot rollout, organizational calendar, and senior leadership input.

▶ The KM officer or learning professional requests budgetary guidelines so these can be taken into consideration for marketing and promotion of the KM system.

▶ The KM project team polls pilot users to create a list of the most useful features and tools of the system. These features can be highlighted in communications to the organization.

▶ Communication specialists on the KM team—such as marketing representatives and learning professionals—create articles that give general information on the upcoming KM system or "teaser advertising" that hints that a new program is coming. They will place these in

Figure 6-3. Questions to Ask When Circulating Knowledge

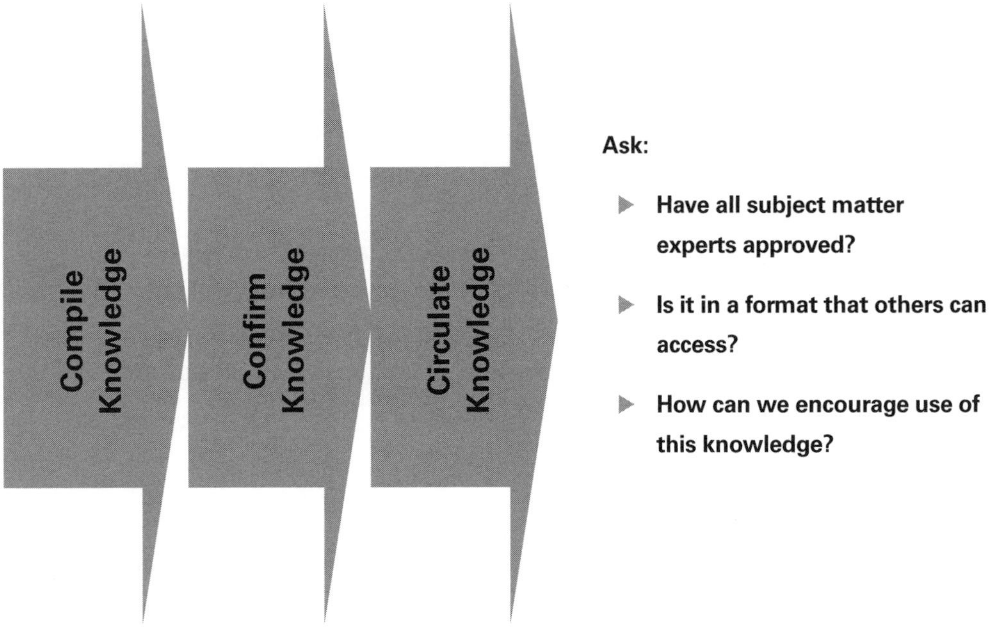

Compile Knowledge

Confirm Knowledge

Circulate Knowledge

Ask:

▶ **Have all subject matter experts approved?**

▶ **Is it in a format that others can access?**

▶ **How can we encourage use of this knowledge?**

existing communication vehicles, such as newsletters, and on the current intranet homepage to build interest for the rollout.

▶ Members of the KM team are given the responsibility to create fact sheets that outline system features and benefits. These can be in the form of handouts to be used at a kickoff event or job aids that can be attached to computer monitors or walls.

▶ Marketing representatives are solicited to request a logo or branding to make the KM system part of the organizational culture. The logo will be used on merchandise, posters, and the homepage of the organization's intranet.

▶ The KM team schedules the kickoff event to introduce the KM system. This event can include an overview by senior leadership, testimonials by pilot users, and a hands-on training session by learning professionals. Additional features may include prizes and branded merchandise.

▶ Learning professionals' duties move to the forefront at this point as they schedule additional training sessions and workshops to ensure that all members of the organization have an opportunity to learn how to access the knowledge base.

▶ All KM team members are assigned specific areas of the KM system where they will monitor activity and encourage discussion.

▶ Through surveys, interviews, and appearances at staff meetings, KM team members immediately begin to solicit success stories and recommendations to be used in follow-up communications.

These are basic steps that will prove beneficial to any KM rollout. The KM officer and team will want to incorporate additional steps that help make the system more appealing to their specific organizational culture. They also will want to discuss the rollout continually with employees at all levels of the organization to ensure that the messages are being received in a positive manner.

Getting It Done

Think about and answer these questions:

1. What are the templates your KM team needs to create for the input of knowledge into the system?
2. What should the standards of quality for knowledge base listings include?
3. Who are the authorities who will validate information from the different areas of the organization?
4. What additional features could be added to your organization's KM system rollout?
5. What is the preliminary timeline for the events of your KM system rollout?

7

Maintaining the KM System

What's Inside This Chapter

In this chapter, you'll learn

▶ How to create follow-up activities to encourage knowledge sharing
▶ How to evaluate your knowledge management system and assess activity
▶ How to revise and update the system.

Knowledge is dynamic. It constantly changes, grows, and eventually becomes obsolete. To ensure continued use of your organization's knowledge database, both the system and the knowledge in it must be upgraded regularly. Although the system processes and formats will stay basically the same, the content will be revised, enhanced, deleted, and freshened for as long as the system lasts. It's the only way to keep users engaged in contributing to and accessing what's housed there.

A system maintenance plan is imperative if your knowledge management system is going to remain a valuable organization resource. Initiatives such as one to develop a KM system are not very exciting when they've been in place for a while. They can become virtually invisible, and it's up to you and your KM project team to maintain the integrity and usefulness of the system and to bring people's attention to it whenever possible.

In this chapter, we'll look at methods to ensure updates, promote traffic to and through the database, and evaluate and improve the whole KM system.

Think About This

Knowledge management behaviors need to be embedded in daily business practices, not treated as optional activities, for the program to become established in an organization.

Who Owns the Knowledge Management Function?

Your KM project team guides the knowledge management efforts of your organization to ensure that they stay true to the goals of the program, and it plays a vital role in promoting the submission of information and the use of the knowledge gathered and housed in the system. But just as the knowledge in an organization doesn't reside with only one department, neither does the ownership of and responsibility for knowledge belong to one group. As an enterprise-wide venture, this system must be the responsibility of everyone in the organization who holds, generates, and uses the knowledge.

Some organizations have found that appointing a chief knowledge officer (CKO), knowledge management officer (KMO), chief learning officer (CLO), or some similar dedicated position has been vital to maintain the momentum and consistency of KM efforts. This role differs from that of a chief information officer (CIO), who focuses on the technological needs of the organization. The CKO/KMO/CLO maximizes the creation, discovery, and dissemination of knowledge, focusing on productivity and profitability by driving the adoption of effective knowledge use in the organization. His or her responsibilities may include providing guidance and drafting policy on ways to institutionalize KM practices, promoting the KM vision and an understanding of the system at all organization levels, developing metrics and standards of practice, monitoring compliance with those standards, and ensuring that the system stays true to its purpose and to the organization's strategic goals. In most cases, the CKO/CLO reports directly to the chief executive officer.

Users and contributors to the system also should be viewed as owners of knowledge management for the organization, as should the monitors, members of the communities of practice, and subject matter experts who continually validate new information and update current listings. By stressing and promoting an organizationwide ownership of the system, your KM team will begin to instill the trust and pride needed to ensure the continuing use and updating of the knowledge housed there.

Think About This

According to a survey conducted by *Knowledge Management Magazine* and International Data Corporation about the state of KM (Dyer and McDonough, 2001), the primary business uses of KM are to

1. capture and share best practices
2. provide training and corporate learning
3. manage customer relationships
4. deliver competitive intelligence
5. provide project workspace.

Follow-up Activities to the KM Launch

After the pilot testing and initial launch of the system, interest in it will drop off. Your knowledge officer or KM team will need to plan and implement activities to stimulate interest, remind content contributors to update their submissions, and encourage employees (and customers, when that's appropriate) to use the system and offer feedback.

The promotional activities that will work best are ones that match your organization's culture and its goals for the KM system. Here are some ideas:

▶ Send an email every six months to remind individuals of their importance to the KM system and to ask them to take time to review and update their materials.

▶ Include a section in new employee orientation on how to use the knowledge base.

▶ Send out highlights newsletters with recently updated information that may be useful to others in the organization.

▶ Hold recognition and reward events that spotlight outstanding individual contributors, communities of practice, networks, or teams.

▶ Include hyperlinks or contact information in knowledge base listings (remember the yellow pages format?) to give credit to subject matter experts and make it easy to reach people who have useful information that may not be part of the system.

▶ Send out examples of interesting questions that have been posted so that knowledge holders will be prompted to submit their answers.

▶ Create training sessions of best practices compiled from the knowledge base.

▶ Encourage communities of practice to develop their individuality and create methods to promote their missions.

▶ If people are not adding content to the knowledge base, consider holding a competition for new entries.

▶ Enlist a department that encounters problems with workplace processes, such as an accounting department that can't get employees to fill out their expense reports correctly. Work directly with them to compile the information and publicize the posting of the information.

▶ Identify recurring challenges that workers are experiencing and send out communications that explain where ideas and answers that address those problems are located in the KM system.

▶ Create a new intranet homepage that is updated frequently to include new "knowledge notes" and other tips from the knowledge base.

▶ When a question is asked repeatedly or knowledge is discovered that can be of use to a large number of people in the organization, add it to a frequently asked question list and post the list on the intranet homepage.

▶ Regularly review your new knowledge base listings for information that you can add to your existing training and development programs. Highlight that information for your learners and identify its location in the KM system .

▶ Hold KM training sessions with tips and techniques that can make searches faster and more efficient.

▶ Use information from the knowledge base to create new training and development classes, and then indicate where this and additional information can be found so that learners are encouraged to visit the database if they have more questions.

The goal of promoting the KM system beyond its initial launch is to drive traffic to it. This requires the KM officer or team to put on a "marketing hat" and think of creative methods to advertise the system—methods that range from events and innovative communications to promotional merchandise.

Noted

Shahar Harel of the Goddard Space Flight Center popularized the story of how, during the 1960s, NASA decided it needed a ballpoint pen to write in the zero-gravity environment of its space capsules. After considerable research and development, the Astronaut Pen was developed at a cost of about $1 million. The pen worked well in space and enjoyed modest success as a novelty item back on earth.

The Soviet Union, faced with the same problem, used a pencil.

The moral of the story is that effectively applying knowledge merely to create novel solutions is not sufficient. Creating and applying knowledge may merely add time and cost unless it produces something of distinct value to the marketplace or to the organization.

– Michael H. Zack, "Competing on Knowledge"

Basic Rule 7
Knowledge continually must be updated, revised, and built on to maintain a valid base.

Assessments and Evaluations of the KM System

After the initial rollout of the KM system, chances are that traffic will slow down. That's natural. But a key aspect of maintaining the KM system is ensuring that any reduction in traffic is not the result of problems in the system, lack of relevant updated information, or difficulties inputting or accessing information.

Even before the launch, a schedule of periodic system evaluations should be established. These evaluations will include assessments of how extensively the system is being used, how frequently new contributions are added, what users need and if those needs are being answered by the system's content, and how recommended improvements can be accomplished.

Getting reliable information about what your users need now that the system is in operation entails much the same process as getting information on users' needs during the development phase. It demands that the KM team survey the users through interviews and written or online surveys. Here are some questions to consider:

▶ How useful do you find the information in the KM database?
▶ How clear is the information you've reviewed?
▶ Is it easy or difficult to locate information you need?
▶ Do you search for more than one item at a time?
▶ Do you generally find what you're looking for?
▶ How long is your average search time?
▶ If you contribute information to the system, do you find it easy or difficult to input the data?
▶ If you contribute information, what prompts you to do so?
▶ If you don't contribute information, why is that?
▶ What other information would you like to see included in the KM system?

▶ What other resources would be useful (weblinks, forms, listings)?

▶ Would you recommend this database to other employees? Why or why not?

▶ Would you encourage other employees to contribute information? Why or why not?

▶ Do you have suggestions or ideas for improvements to the system?

If you opt for a written survey, resist the urge to make it too long and involved. It's better to send out a short list of five to 10 questions every few months than to conduct a census-like survey annually. Make the questions easy to answer, using rating scales and check boxes where possible. Simple surveys will generate more responses than will more complex questionnaires. For more in-depth fact finding, it can be effective to invite a focus group of knowledge base users to meet with KM project team representatives to discuss specific benefits and drawbacks of the system. On the simple periodic surveys, ask respondents if they'd be interested in participating in such a focus group.

Revisions and Improvements to the KM System

Knowledge contributors and system monitors are responsible for the content they post, and the knowledge officer ensures that the database in which they post it is operating correctly and answering the needs of users. Periodic meetings of the KM project team should be held to review recommendations and complaints and decide which ones need to be addressed.

Think About This

Whereas continuous revisions and improvements are essential to keep the KM initiative fresh, equally important is allowing flexibility for the unexpected directions the systems may take. For example, the British Broadcasting Corporation (BBC) discovered that its bulletin board played host to more than just discussions of work questions. There were daily life issues and even discussions about shows the BBC had aired. The result? An amazing 450,000 page views a month from 8,000 unique users—in an organization of 25,000.

There is always the possibility that the system designed and implemented by the KM project team may be too advanced for your organization. In that case, it may be necessary to conceal some of the features and allow employees to start out by becoming comfortable with an abridged version of the ultimate system. Perhaps the homepage could be designed to look more like something they've been comfortable with in the past. Perhaps the users could turn features on or off to engage with the system at a level that fits their understanding of and comfort with technology. Or more training workshops could be presented that outline step-by-step instructions for accessing materials and the methods for submitting knowledge to the system.

As the system becomes more widely used, renegade communities of practice or online forums might appear. If they duplicate the efforts of existing forums or are negative in nature, this should be addressed by the KM officer. If they are useful, consider them a benefit of the system's organic format. But don't let the number of networks grow too large because these communities add to the time that KM team members must spend monitoring online activities. Those monitoring the forums can be overwhelmed and unable to review all new material. When reviews are compromised and inaccurate information is included in the knowledge base, the system will lose credibility.

Although it's important to build flexibility into the system and encourage knowledge sharing (the whole purpose), it's equally wise to enforce guidelines and set limits to ensure that quality—not quantity—is the key component of the knowledge housed there.

If a majority of users are adding knowledge to the system but few are searching it for help or answers to questions and problems, the KM team will want to take a fresh look at how the system operates to determine if it's too difficult to search and do a spot-review of the content to see if the information is too basic or too complex to be useful. This would be the time to interview people who *aren't* using the system. Learn what's keeping them out, and take action to correct that. And when problems have been corrected, announce it to the organization so that members know their concerns were addressed.

In your role as a knowledge officer or learning professional, you now will meet regularly with the IT department, the KM project team, mentors, and the organization's senior managers to review challenges, recommendations, and options for updates and additional training. These meetings will look for results from the KM system, such as enhanced productivity through additional collaboration and problem solutions, and processes streamlined by knowledge sharing and wider use of best practices. These sessions also will seek to discover any cost savings realized through improved operations, faster response and turnaround times, and efficiency gains resulting from faster information retrieval and fewer redundant processes.

By continually reviewing the content and process quality of the KM system, the extent to which it's used, and the business results that are evident and measurable, your KM team can ensure that the system continues to satisfy the needs of your organization and fulfill the goals established at the beginning of the development initiative.

Noted

Knowledge is the new capital, but it's worthless unless it's accessible, communicated, and enhanced.

– Hamilton Beazley, Strategic Leadership Group

Getting It Done

Think about and answer these questions:

1. Who is responsible for each area of the KM system, and what are his or her responsibilities?
2. What specific issues will be addressed in the after-action review of the KM system rollout?
3. What follow-up activities would work well for your organization?
4. Which questions should be asked and what standards should be addressed at regular evaluation meetings for the KM system?
5. What additional questions could be included in a survey of the users of the KM system?

8

KM Resources and Tools

 What's Inside This Chapter

In this chapter, you'll find

▶ Features and factors to consider in planning and developing technology for a KM system
▶ Help in deciding if external assistance is needed
▶ A Microsoft PowerPoint presentation for explaining knowledge management to your organization.

In this chapter, we'll consider resources and tools the KM development team can use while putting the system together and promoting it to the organization. The team should be using the same information-search systems to research KM systems as those that will be established in the organization's new KM system. The networks that will provide the information to accomplish this project are knowledge management systems in themselves. You and the development team aren't trying to reinvent the cotton gin or be process pioneers. There are myriad resources and tools to help create your organization's KM system, and many can be found by entering the term *knowledge management* in your favorite web search engine. Your team is looking for best practices; what has and hasn't worked for others; resources, KM software recommendations, and quick tips; and answers to "What would you do differently knowing what you know now?" If sharing and building on knowledge is the overall purpose of all knowledge management efforts, why shouldn't you and the development team approach the project with exactly that intention and through precisely that process?

If your project team members can maintain open minds while participating in the KM initiative development, they can create a system that wisely incorporates the experience and lessons that others have learned in devising and implementing ways to manage organizational knowledge—while still uniquely suited to the business and culture of your organization.

The reference section at the back of this book lists books, articles, and websites that offer more in-depth information and help in designing, launching, and maintaining an effective and successful KM system. And, there are so many other resources within communities of practice and professional groups in your organization's industry. Take advantage of their experiences and insights.

Software

It's not necessary to start this system with a dedicated software package, but it definitely will be an investment the organization will want to consider at some point in the process. Here are some factors and activities your KM team or knowledge officer can consider when making a decision on software:

- ▶ Focus on the goals set for the system. Instead of coming up with an expansive wish list, describe some sample situations in which members of the organization would use the software to try to answer questions or solve problems. Now describe how the organization currently handles those situations. Decide where the software could offer an advantage and what improvements could be expected in the way things are done as a result of using KM software.
- ▶ Talk with people in similar organizations who have used software solutions. Find out how satisfied they are with the software choices

they made (or were handed), and ask what challenges they've encountered.

▶ Conduct online searches and use trial demonstrations to discover additional features that might be useful to the organization.

▶ Ask vendors for software information and suggestions, but don't schedule onsite demonstrations until the team has narrowed its choices and is ready to move forward. Don't waste your time and that of the vendors.

▶ Ask open-ended questions when you speak with vendors. Instead of asking, "Does your software offer collaborative workspaces?" ask, "How does your software support collaborative workflow?" Open-ended questions will prompt more expansive and informative answers and will tell you if the vendor knows more than what's printed on the product feature sheet.

▶ When scheduling a vendor presentation, make it clear that you want the vendor to use the organization's real-world scenarios in her or his demonstrations. You're not interested in watching canned Power-Point examples that aren't pertinent to the work taking place daily in various areas of the organization.

▶ Ask technical staff and people who are likely to be regular users of the KM system to attend demonstrations and ask questions that are relevant to their practice areas or concerns.

▶ Take nothing for granted. Discover if there are performance modules, optional subprograms, or ancillary hardware that will have to be purchased to make the standard software package run well and accomplish what the organization needs.

▶ When you've made a selection and purchase of software, it's often worthwhile to send a few staff members to a class at the vendor's training center. Equip them with real-world problems or projects to address in the training class.

By taking the time to research thoroughly and assess available software systems before making that big investment, your organization can find the system that makes the most sense for its needs, preferences, and resources.

Intranet, Extranet, and Internet

Your organization probably uses an intranet in some manner, even if not to its fullest extent. Your KM project team should meet with members of the IT department to learn about the network. Ask about their experiences and challenges working with it as an indicator for the problems the KM system may encounter there.

It's possible that the organization's intranet has the beginnings of a KM system already in place and that the IT professionals have done some knowledge management research. They'll be priceless resources and development team members. Talk to the IT people about the design of the organization's intranet, extranet, and Internet homepages, tabs, folders, and search features that could support the KM system even before or without an investment in new software.

Internal versus External Resources

Here's a question that always is asked at some point in the system development process: "Do we need a consultant to do this?" The basic answer is *no,* as long as the organization is willing and has the resources to form and support a development team dedicated (at least part time) to researching, planning, and guiding the project all the way through its full-scale rollout. However, a competent, knowledgeable, and relevantly experienced consultant (with demonstrable successes in KM planning) can help speed up the initial planning stages during which the team is getting its bearings, can steer the team in the right direction throughout the development phases, and serve as calendar- and timekeeper to maintain task focus.

To ensure that the chosen consultant can answer the team's needs, do some research. Talk with people from other organizations that have used consultants. Study companies with systems that could serve as models for your organization's system, and ask if they used a specific consultant. Find out what KM projects the consultants have done before and contact their references. If you're considering a larger consulting group, ask who in the consultancy will be handling your project and learn that person's KM track record. And perhaps most important, hold a few meetings with potential consultants to assess their fit with the development team and with the organization.

Carefully define how extensively the team will use the consultant's services. Will he help only at the beginning to get the team started? Will she serve on a long-term basis from start to rollout? Describe the scope of services in writing and make certain everyone involved knows what is and isn't included in the contract. Finally, define the expected length of service and optional termination points so all parties have a clear understanding of consultancy duration.

Basic Rule 8

Knowledge management systems must use the principles they encourage—sharing, cooperation, and continual growth.

Online Communities

Numerous online communities offer discussions of KM best prctices and ask questions of those who've gone through this experience. For example, pages on the American Society for Training & Development (ASTD) discussion boards (www.community.astd.org) offer areas where ASTD members can post questions and hold conversations on virtually any training topic. This is knowledge sharing in action.

To find additional online communities, a simple search for the keyword *knowledge management* in a web search engine can connect you to the latest active listings—including some outstanding college programs and resource sites, both nonprofit and commercial. Additionally, a visit to the major blog communities using the same keyword will reveal authors, consultants, and companies who specialize in knowledge management.

Additional Resources for KM Rollouts

Two of the biggest challenges the KM development team will face in the first steps of the initiative are increasing the organization's awareness of knowledge management and getting people to understand why and how such a system will be valuable to them. To help you with this part of the initiative,

this book includes access to a PowerPoint presentation that you may down-
load at http://www.astd.org/knowledgemanagementbasics. This presentation can be used first to give an overview of KM to the senior management
of the organization. Without their support and dedication of resources, a KM
initiative cannot be sustained. The presentation also can be used as part of
KM workforce orientation sessions to help allay any fears employees might
have and to give them a first view of the benefits a KM system could hold for
them. Addressing their question, "What's in it for me?" at the beginning of the
initiative could help gain acceptance for the KM process and make employees more willing to share knowledge. A script for use with the PowerPoint
slides is included in Appendix B.

Tools 8-1, 8-2, and 8-3 offer additional help at different stages of the KM
development process. Tool 8-1 is a form to use when compiling knowledge
sources existing in the organization. Tool 8-2 is a place to compile the
names of knowledge owners and monitors for all the content areas the final
system will contain. It also offers space to record a detailed process plan for
having knowledge reviewed. Tool 8-3 will be useful when the development
team is choosing among a number of potential knowledge-sharing formats.
Use the form to list the advantages and disadvantages of each format being
considered.

KM Tools for the Development Team

In the true sense of knowledge management as a sharing of expert knowledge and experience, people who already have gone through this process
are great resources who can share their successes and roadblocks and give
your KM team the benefit of the lessons they've learned along the way. Use
professional associations, best-practices roundtables, conferences, and contacts with peers to learn from others' experiences. Partner informally with
people who are about to go through the same process so your KM team can
collaborate on research with a community of practice. Invite those who
have completed the process to join your team in peer assists.

Collaborative tools can be useful devices for learning from others and for
conducting the operations of the KM project team. These are computer-based
applications that enable individuals to work together and share information
even at great distances. Examples include professional and social networking

Tool 8-1. Current Knowledge Sources

Instructions: Use this form to list any knowledge sources that currently exist in your organization. Consider knowledge in all formats, from hard copies of manuals and books, to online resources, to people who are experts in or beyond their areas of effort. An example is provided in the first row.

Format	Location	Types of Knowledge	Owner/ Monitor	Notes and Comments
Management blog	*Internet: Link on homepage*	*Information on strategic planning, new developments, current challenges*	*CEO CEO's executive assistant*	*Updated weekly or as needed*

Tool 8-2. Monitors to Confirm the Knowledge

Instructions: Use this form to list knowledge topics, knowledge sources or owners, people who are responsible for validating the information from that source, and the steps for reviewing and confirming that specific knowledge. An example is provided in the first row.

Topic	Knowledge Owner	Knowledge Monitor	Knowledge Review Method
Accounting policies	*CFO*	*Accounting manager*	▶ *Email new information to accounting manager, with confirmation of receipt* ▶ *Accounting manager distributes to finance and accounting directors* ▶ *Directors respond to accounting manager* ▶ *Accounting manager sends original information and responses to CFO* ▶ *CFO makes changes, signs off, and routes back to accounting manager* ▶ *Accounting manager reviews and updates information every six months*

Tool 8-3. Pros and Cons of Knowledge-Sharing Formats Being Considered

Instructions: Use this form to record and then compare the benefits and challenges of various knowledge-sharing formats. Some commonly used formats are listed and described in the first two columns; add others as desired. Completing the form will help you choose among or prioritize possible formats for your KM system.

Format	Description	Benefits	Challenges	Notes and Comments
After-action review	*Session held after a project or event to analyze process and outcomes*			
Blog	*Online journal of news and events*			
Training classes	*Training modules covered in traditional classroom settings, online training, or mobile (mp3, web) training formats*			
Communities of practice	*Groups of people with similar goals who learn through social networking platforms*			
Intranet	*Company's electronic storehouse of information*			
Manuals	*Written or electronic documents*			
Wiki	*Database of information that users can edit and link to other sources of information*			

sites that can help locate people and groups with common interests, productivity applications, online calendars, presentation-sharing sites, bulletin boards, instant messaging, whiteboards, audio and/or video conferencing, discussion groups, and search engines that can help locate relevant documents and knowledge sources.

Using as many of the tools of knowledge management as you can will help you ensure that you have the most current and relevant information to use in making decisions about your KM system.

Think About This

A vast storehouse of knowledge already exists in your organization. It's the goal of KM efforts to make that knowledge accessible to others so that it can become the basis for informed decisions, improved operations, and tomorrow's innovations.

Getting It Done

Think about and answer these questions:

1. Does the organization already have KM tools in place?
2. If not, what are the features that would be required of a KM software solution for the organization?
3. How could the organization use current resources to house its knowledge base?
4. Would your organization benefit from an external resource to assist in its KM efforts?
5. What sites can you visit on the Internet to learn from others' KM experiences?

9

Best Practices in KM

What's Inside This Chapter

In this chapter, you'll find

▶ Best practices from organizations currently practicing KM
▶ Recommendations and counsel from KM practitioners
▶ Lessons learned from experience with knowledge management.

It's encouraging to see that companies worldwide are recognizing and reaping the benefits of KM practices. And though the organizations vary in the amount of resources they can devote to knowledge-sharing activities, their efforts have generated a wealth of best-practices literature that they've not been shy about sharing.

In this chapter, we'll consider best practices for specific areas of KM and analyze the lessons others have learned so we can avoid some of the stumbling blocks that people and companies have encountered when developing and implementing their KM systems.

Basic Rule 9

No single knowledge management system will work for every organization.

Best Practices in Knowledge-Sharing Incentives

It's unrealistic to expect employees to share knowledge automatically just because a KM system has been put in place. After years of operating under the principle that knowledge is power, thinking that they're too busy to share knowledge, and watching their managers hoard knowledge, employees typically aren't in a hurry to share what they know. So an organization often needs to consider incentives for employees—lures to draw them into the system and encourage their contributions to and use of the knowledge available there. Here are some ideas:

▶ One helpful activity is a culture shift that includes obvious changes in leaders' behavior. Getting executives to vocally and behaviorally champion knowledge sharing and to take the lead by using the KM tools as soon as they're available has been found very effective in getting employees intrigued and willing to become part of the knowledge-sharing community.

▶ Holding private sessions to help leaders understand and use the tools effectively will enable them to become stronger champions of the KM system from the outset. Additionally, helping them produce some of the first submissions to the knowledge base sends a strong message of support to middle and frontline management.

▶ Publicize—in print, online, and in person—the role models who are contributing to or effectively using the KM system. These role models may include leaders of the organization as mentioned earlier, and you should recognize longtime employees, respected members of the organization, and even new recruits who immediately embrace the KM system.

- ▶ Regularly allocate time at staff meetings and team events to share knowledge and offer suggestions for improvements.
- ▶ Create team competitions so that knowledge sharing becomes a unifying, rather than divisive element in departments. Instead of giving individual rewards, these competitions reward the teams of people who submit, use, or build on the knowledge base.
- ▶ Recruit subject matter experts to submit a specified number of entries to the knowledge base. Encourage their participation by making their entries a means to earn points toward an annual bonus.
- ▶ Create a competition in which project teams design new ways to perform outdated processes. Form cross-departmental teams with diverse areas of expertise or simply announce the process to be updated and encourage people to form teams on their own.
- ▶ Establish a practice of recognizing or rewarding different knowledge-related accomplishments. For example, reward the person who returns from a conference or workshop and contributes knowledge that the department considers most useful. Depending on the frequency with which employees attend such gatherings, poll the department members quarterly or every six months to learn what they believe has been most useful in their work. Another option is to create a forum for people to report how they've used information from the knowledge base and then appoint a committee to review and recognize outstanding reports.
- ▶ Include employees' knowledge-sharing practices in the performance management system and add them as criteria to be considered in performance appraisals.
- ▶ Build knowledge sharing into daily business processes. For example, create templates that allow immediate recording of information or questions from phone calls, customer situations, or equipment or product issues. These templates can be online, by email, or even paper based, if necessary.
- ▶ Reinforce the equal importance of gaining knowledge and sharing it by including stories of successful use of the knowledge base in newsletters, emails, organizational meetings, and new employee orientations.

Best Practices in System Rollout

The initial rollout of a KM system includes the essential activities of communication and training, but there are other considerations that can help make the introduction of the program successful.

▶ Some organizations have learned the difficult lesson of not being over-ambitious in their initial KM efforts. They tried to show their strong commitment to knowledge management by embarking on large-scale projects at the outset. They built extensive databases—and then discovered that the systems overwhelmed their employees. People were reluctant to use them. Knowledge officers realized they had to step back and rethink their KM strategies.

▶ Most companies have found that it works best to start with one receptive area of the organization to pilot test a program. They select a department with a supportive manager who is open to the concepts of KM, and they work with the department to identify one process that could be improved with better access to current company knowledge. They address this with the simplest possible KM solution as a test for the system. Then they have the opportunity to work out any problems before the system is offered to a larger portion of the workforce.

▶ Although many KM systems attract a great deal of interest and initial browsing, some KM practitioners warn that it can take time for regular use to be incorporated into daily practices. They note that the KM team should continue planned promotions and not be discouraged by slow response because it takes time to create new habits.

Best Practices in Contact Databases

Many organizations have added directories of their subject matter experts to their intranets, and those directories become popular tools in networking among individuals who normally would have no opportunity for contact.

▶ The directory page for each expert may contain a business card, information about internal and external associates and networks, a résumé and list of areas of expertise, a list of organizations to which the person belongs, a list of languages spoken, and a calendar of appointments and events. Tags and key words are included on each page to make it easy for a person seeking specific expertise to locate the right people. To keep the information fresh and current, organization members with pages get regular email reminders to update their listings.

▶ Allowing in the contact database such personal touches as favorite weblinks, a description of hobbies, audio and video clips, and photographs has encouraged employees to consult experts because people are inclined to talk more easily if they can see the face of the person they're speaking with or if they have something in common with the expert. For example, the KM team at BP created a yellow pages directory on the company intranet—BP Amoco Connect. The site attracted 10,000 users in its first year, and four years later the number of users had risen to 32,000—one third of the entire global workforce.

▶ One challenge to a comprehensive system is the loss of valuable knowledge after phone conversations end between individuals who come into contact through the database. Organizations are learning the value of capturing the knowledge generated or exchanged with such simple means as question-and-answer lists with links for contacting the experts.

Best Practices in KM Activities and Events

KM practitioners have found that it's possible to make knowledge management more accessible to a wide range of employees if they organize and hold a variety of activities. Here are some practices that have worked:

▶ In-person or online knowledge fairs are forums where departments or teams meet to update others on their recent projects and activities, demonstrate knowledge-sharing efforts, and learn from each other.

▶ Although the suggestion box has become outdated, organizations are finding ways to solicit employee input and ideas through such activities as competitions, lunch-and-learn meetings, and roundtable sessions.

▶ Conference calls continue to be popular meeting opportunities, but more organizations are taking advantage of the videoconferencing and of the expanded capabilities offered by technology: online meetings with workspaces for presentations, document viewing, and simultaneous editing of the materials being discussed.

▶ Audio and video records of meetings and learning events make it possible to capture the knowledge generated and shared there and to circulate it to others who weren't able to attend. Carefully editing the audio or video recordings allows the key information to be made into podcasts, short presentations that address different audiences in the organization, and modules that support various types of training.

▶ Additionally, company intranet sites are serving as groupware with server space for project teams and even clients. These sites include chat areas and bulletin boards for online meetings and discussions on selected topics and challenges.

▶ One governmental entity has found a way to take knowledge sharing to the next level before introducing any technology changes. By creating a trainer development program designed especially for subject matter experts, the agency prepared subject matter experts in various departments to share their knowledge with others. To complete the program, each participant designed a class to present to his or her departments. These classes were submitted for posting to the online class database so that other departments could use any relevant information from the training programs. In this way, a small training department has expanded knowledge management efforts across the entire agency and is capturing knowledge for others to use and build on. This knowledge base will become a foundation for the KM system when it's instituted, thus creating an instant collection of knowledge already reviewed and validated.

▶ A nonprofit organization has created an effective KM system with a unique personality. National Novel Writing Month (www.NaNoWriMo.org) began in 1999 with 21 writers who decided to complete a novel in one month's time. In November 2007, NaNoWriMo hosted more than 100,000 participants from more than 70 countries. Each person attempted to write a 50,000-word novel in one month. Online forums enabled idea sharing, question answering, problem solving, and camaraderie as the deadline approached. Podcasts were posted to motivate participants. Word counts and information were updated continually. Many writers decided to meet face-to-face in their regions for writing sessions and workshops, but people who couldn't meet in person got encouragement, information, and a sense of community from the online activities and events.

Noted

Knowledge is not a dead pile of facts, but on the contrary, the outcome of a dynamic interaction with the world at large, and most importantly, with the other people in it.

– Stowe Boyd, CKO, Knowledge Capital Group

Best Practices Among Communities of Practice

Communities of practice are proving their worth as resources to generate additional knowledge in an organization. These communities typically are able to combine the social aspects that appeal to those who prefer direct contact with others and the ease of use associated with online networking. The growing acceptance of networking sites—LinkedIn, MySpace, and Facebook—has made online communities more familiar to members of the workforce, allowing for easier adoption as a workplace tool.

Here are some of the best practices identified by productive communities of practice:

▶ To start a community, be sure to invite a few members with good communication skills to keep the conversations active.

▶ Agree on a defined purpose and charter as soon as the community has been formed and is getting acquainted.

▶ Limit the size to keep the community manageable and, if necessary, split the community into subsets to make room for additional members.

▶ Enlist a good moderator to identify issues, monitor and enforce boundaries, and energize conversations.

▶ Poll members regularly to be sure they want to remain in the group.

▶ Hold occasional face-to-face meetings to support the social side of the communities and encourage comfortable conversation.

- ▶ Leave messages on the discussion board for a set period and then archive them. Sixty days was cited as a maximum by most of the communities polled.
- ▶ Consider cultivating communities outside the organization—including customers and vendors—in which you can gather additional information, conduct informal surveys and discussions, and promote customer involvement and loyalty.

Best Practices When Involving External Customers

Retail and service companies are finding that their customers can be served more efficiently when the KM system includes portals through which customers can get to user manuals, troubleshooting charts, technical support services, and even videos that demonstrate proper maintenance and additional ideas for using the products they've purchased. These organizations have reduced the number of technical support calls they receive and so are able to decrease the number of employees in their call centers.

- ▶ In many cases, companies already have Internet sites and their resource pages on those sites included product information. That meant the main revisions needed to create useful customer resources were simplifying language and making the site more user friendly so that customers could navigate and locate information easily. Companies have discovered that resulting savings in time spent on service phone calls have more than offset the costs of revising the information systems.
- ▶ Companies have discovered that creating customer focus groups helps increase customer involvement and loyalty. They invite customers to serve in advisory positions by creating bulletin boards where customers can post ideas and suggestions. The companies also use the bulletin boards to request customer input on product and service issues.
- ▶ Simple pop-up surveys on the company's Internet site have been found to be a valuable tool for gathering additional information, feedback, and insights from existing and potential customers.

Lessons Learned

Organizations that have imagined, designed, developed, implemented, and maintained systems to manage their knowledge have learned valuable lessons, and any organization on that same path can benefit from the accumulated wisdom of experience. Here are some general lessons learned:

▸ All three KM elements—people, processes, and technology—must be considered when developing knowledge management plans. When the system leans too heavily on technology, its potential for success is limited if people don't adapt to that technology. When it depends completely on people, the system may fail if its main champions leave the organization. And if the KM system focuses only on processes and ignores the end users or the maintenance of knowledge housed in the technology, it won't be useful to the people it was designed to support.

▸ Incorporating several knowledge-sharing formats into the system will encourage its use by more members of the organization. Just as individuals learn in different ways, they also differ in the ways they respond to types of technology, social situations, and methods of connectivity and communication. Whereas some employees may adapt easily to wikis and interactive online tools, others may need simpler and more basic tools to avoid being overwhelmed by the system. For example, socializing and sharing information face-to-face is essential for some people to become comfortable with a KM system. Once they're acclimated, they can venture into the other formats available in the system.

▸ Don't ignore bottom-up, or self-organizing, knowledge-sharing networks that sprout organically in the organization. Nurture them and give them the tools they need to grow. A series of posts on a bulletin board can reveal areas of interest or need that the organization didn't know existed. An observant KM team can help the people who've made the posts organize into a community of practice to continue their discussions in a dedicated location.

▸ Virtual communities should be encouraged and supported with chat tools, online bulletin boards, and means for disseminating newsletters and audiovisual updates.

▸ Knowledge management systems are prompting gains in e-business for organizations making successful use of their KM initiatives. Faster market and turnaround times, new product and service offerings, and better activities coordination are responsible for the business boost.

▶ An organization that takes its KM function seriously creates a position to lead and coordinate the function. Chief knowledge officer and knowledge management officer are two of the most common titles for this position (and there should be no confusion with the chief information officer, who leads the company's technology initiatives). This position is responsible for communicating the value of knowledge and promoting the concept of knowledge management to the organization. Additionally, the CKO oversees the step-by-step processes of development, implementation, and maintenance of the KM system.

▶ Organizations that effectively coordinate KM with the learning function create additional opportunities for the personal and professional development of employees. These opportunities can include such tools as online training sessions, organization charts with qualifications and competency listings for positions, recommendations for developmental activities, and online forums allowing meetings with mentors.

Best Practices for the Un-Teched

Technological solutions and software systems make creating and maintaining KM systems easier than doing it all on paper, but they're not the only methods of communicating that knowledge. Personal interaction still has its place in the sharing of knowledge, with coaching, on-the-job training, and mentoring, as well as fundamental tools such as manuals, instruction cards, posters, and other written methods.

Successful KM practitioners have found some frontline employees afraid to use the tools. They realized that provisions must be made to bring the advantages of organizational knowledge to those fearful or hesitant workers. Their blended systems now enable both personal and software-based access to knowledge.

▶ Long-standing techniques for sharing knowledge can be just as effective as the latest e-whatever. Teamwork, process management, benchmarking, and face-to-face meetings still can get the job done.

▶ Technology and online collaboration doesn't eliminate the need for in-person meetings, although it can make it easier and less expensive when there is no viable way to bring bodies together in the same room. People still need contact with one another to build trust, foster open communication, and share tacit knowledge. Where it's possible to meet in person, at least occasionally, make that happen. Where cost, schedules, or extreme distances make it unfeasible, online video-conferencing creates the next-best meeting space.

I recall the days when I was managing knowledge and didn't know it—when there was little or no "technology" involved. One of the first knowledge management projects I worked on was a supervisor handbook. (Of course I'd never heard the term *knowledge management* so I just called it a resource.) Its table of contents was a simple list of frequently asked questions. I solicited questions from supervisors in the company—questions about HR procedures, office equipment procurement, safety practices, and more. (In effect, the contents served as the portal to all the information in the handbook.) I gathered the questions into topic areas and created tables of questions and the brief answers. In columns next to the tables, I listed the company's major resources—HR handbook, company operations manual, products catalog, and the employee handbook—and noted where in those resources a more complete answer could be found for every question. In that way, I created a single resource that housed information on an array of subjects that didn't have to be updated every time minor revisions were made to a procedure. The major resource documents could change, but the unchanged supervisor handbook still directed users to the complete and current information.

As time went on and I became more technology savvy (or thought I was at the time), I replaced the printed supervisor handbook with an online document that included hyperlinks to the major resources and other useful ancillary materials.

Most people will view this process for creating the original supervisor handbook as closely akin to chiseling on a stone tablet, but it was a successful knowledge management system for the organization. It worked. And it can still work for organizations that need immediate, low- or no-tech solutions for knowledge sharing.

Just as knowledge is always changing, so should the formats, information, and KM activities reflect the changing skill levels and developments in the world of knowledge sharing. Refer to the references in the back of this book as a starting place to find the newest best practices and lessons learned.

On the web there are multitudes of communities that share best practices in knowledge management. Those organizations also can help learning professionals identify other groups at the same stage of KM planning so they can share experiences based on the latest advances in the field.

Noted

The more extensive a man's knowledge of what has been done, the greater will be his power of knowing what to do.

– Benjamin Disraeli, British statesman

Getting It Done

Think about and answer these questions:

1. Which of the best practices in this chapter would work well for your organization?
2. What are some of the online resources your KM team should use for additional research?
3. Is the position of chief knowledge officer a possibility for your organization?
4. What could you do to encourage the activities and development of communities of practice in your KM system?
5. What low-tech solutions might you want to consider for your organization?

10

The Future of KM

What's Inside This Chapter

In this chapter, you'll find

▶ A review of the basic rules of knowledge management
▶ How to make flexibility part of your system maintenance plan
▶ A glimpse into the future of knowledge management.

In this book, we've looked at a broad variety of goals, practices, and experiments for knowledge management ventures. But trying immediately to create a knowledge management system that's all things to all people is both self-defeating and just frankly impossible.

Keeping in mind the nine Basic Rules we've covered so far as you develop your system can help you build on the best practices of current KM practitioners and help you avoid some of the stumbling blocks they encountered. As a refresher, here are those basic rules again:

1. To be effective, knowledge management must address three essential components—people, process, and technology.

2. Knowledge management systems must engage every department in the organization.

3. An organization first should conduct a needs assessment to determine the goals, scope, and requirements of any knowledge management activities it is considering.

4. Before creating knowledge management systems, the organization should identify existing formal or informal knowledge sources.

5. The design of a knowledge management system should be based on desired results *and* on the organization's culture and expertise.

6. Effective knowledge management systems enable the organization to share its knowledge *and* discover inconsistencies in its knowledge.

7. Knowledge continually must be updated, revised, and built on to maintain a valid base.

8. Knowledge management systems must use the principles they encourage—sharing, cooperation, and continual growth.

9. No single knowledge management system will work for every organization.

This book and continued research on the growing knowledge management movement will help your KM project team decide what's most needed in the organization. Ideally, the KM initiative will start small. And the team wants to keep your organization's KM goals in mind as it selects the most valuable and useful tools and functions for the system and shelve the rest of the ideas for later development.

We can become distracted and drawn in by new concepts. Remember when we thought that online training was the only thing we'd ever need again? When we were certain that a Total Quality Management program would solve every problem an organization could encounter? In the world of training, education, and employee development, there will never be a single, unchanging answer. It's a good thing. We learning professionals would grow bored.

Over the years, one constant aspect of business success is knowledge: the ability to access it, the need to learn from it, and the opportunity to build on it. Knowledge management systems undoubtedly will blossom and morph into something we don't recognize in years to come, but the basic need for the knowledge that drives those systems will remain.

Keeping the KM System Flexible

Never lose sight of the big picture of knowledge management: Your organization is participating in this initiative to contribute to the communication and exchange of knowledge among members of the organization. Devising workable systems for sharing that knowledge must operate in tandem with letting the sharing channels take forms that we didn't foresee.

Communication systems may arise in one-to-one discussions, and unexpected mentoring situations may appear. We may discover that specific processes are being done incorrectly in entire departments. From time to time, forums may go astray and teams may come up with findings that aren't pleasant to hear. Evaluations may force us to rethink the entire system structure. All of these situations—and more that we can't imagine now—will demand flexibility in the system and its team of monitors, designers, and managers.

Knowledge sharing is not a precise business—it's messy. That means we have to support the sharing of knowledge even if it develops outside our carefully planned systems. Part of maintaining a KM system going forward is reviewing new channels and formats that sprout organically among system users and periodically trying to quantify, standardize, and organize the knowledge generated in these ways. Doing so will make the new knowledge more widely available throughout the organization. In the meantime, as the system chugs along, we have to satisfy ourselves with the fact that we've facilitated a culture of knowledge sharing. That was the initial goal, wasn't it?

Looking Forward

With technology constantly changing, it's impossible to judge what future KM software and systems will look like. But it is possible to imagine how KM systems will operate in organizations and how members of the organization and external users will interact with them. Here are a few thoughts:

- ▶ Successful systems will include clearly identified knowledge bases that support specific organizational goals and objectives.
- ▶ Organizations continually will monitor and update both how the system works and the knowledge presented in the database. Learning professionals will be able to incorporate that knowledge into training and development programs.

▶ Leaders will model the knowledge-sharing behaviors that they want to see in their organizations; and with their increased appreciation and understanding of the benefits of KM, they will make even greater investments of organization resources and time in the expanded development and use of KM systems.

▶ Strategic planners will incorporate their organization's KM strategies as key factors in achieving future goals.

▶ Ratings that evaluate an employee's contributions to and use of the database will be part of all performance reviews, and effective sharing and building on knowledge will become a competency that is considered during the recruitment and hiring of future employees.

▶ Communities of practice will become more abundant and turn into major contributors to organizational knowledge and growth. Leaders and noted contributors in those communities will move into roles as trainers and knowledge resources for their organizations.

▶ Innovative knowledge-sharing formats—mp3 downloads, email training, syndicated updates, and much more—will be assessed and integrated into the system.

Noted

Connection, not collection: That's the essence of knowledge management.

– Tom Stewart, The Wealth of Knowledge: Intellectual Capital and the Twenty-first Century Organization

▶ More organizations will recognize the need for knowledge officers and additional learning professional roles, including specific positions for the development and maintenance of knowledge assets.

▶ Learning professionals will instruct subject matter experts to use their knowledge base to create tools like quick tips, troubleshooting guides,

Noted

Knowledge comes, but wisdom lingers.
— Alfred, Lord Tennyson, English poet

and information sheets that make the database user friendly and relevant to all levels of the organization.

▶ Electronic prompts and reminders to share knowledge will be triggered automatically during standard business processes and procedures.

▶ Templates and guidelines will simplify the process of contributing knowledge to the organization's databases, and software systems will automate the processes of validating, formatting, and editing knowledge.

▶ As successful KM systems expand, there will be continued growth and enhancement in

  ▶ mentoring
  ▶ leadership training
  ▶ documents and records management
  ▶ market information and competitive intelligence
  ▶ search-and-find tools
  ▶ lessons learned
  ▶ innovation management
  ▶ identification of subject matter experts
  ▶ workplace design
  ▶ collaboration
  ▶ training and education
  ▶ email management.

That's just a glimpse into the future of knowledge management. The full picture at your organization depends on your goals, your commitment, and your vision.

When your system develops into a best practice of knowledge management, share your story with one of the many online communities of practice so that others can build on your success. After all, that's true knowledge sharing.

Appendix A

Frequently Asked Questions About KM

Some questions come up in most discussions of knowledge management, and here you'll get some basic answers. For questions that might require more in-depth answers, refer to the chapters cited.

What is knowledge management? (chapter 1)

It's gathering and capturing the knowledge in your organization—whether that knowledge is on paper, stored in a computer, or in a person's head—and then making it available so that others can benefit from it and build on it.

But you can't manage knowledge any more than you can manage time, can you? (chapter 1)

That question is the reason that so many people disagree over the term *knowledge management*. It's also been called *knowledge sharing, knowledge integration,* and a host of other names. That's OK. We know what they mean. And although it may not be technically feasible to "manage" knowledge, it's possible to manage the formats it's presented in and the processes and procedures for circulating it. That's what KM systems focus on.

Noted

Knowledge is power, which is why people who had it in the past often tried to make a secret of it. In post-capitalism, power comes from transmitting information to make it productive, not from hiding it.

– Peter F. Drucker, "The Post-Capitalist Executive,"
Managing in a Time of Great Change

Is KM just another buzzword? (chapter 1)

Knowledge management is not just another new initiative or a "flavor of the day." It's a method for organizing what you're already doing so that the knowledge you've accumulated is readily available to the people who need it. KM creates more opportunities for people to share the valuable knowledge that's in their heads.

What difference could KM make for my organization? (chapter 1)

Experience shows you could expect

▶ increased sales
▶ reduced process cycle time
▶ improved resource allocation
▶ increased productivity
▶ reduced employee and customer frustration
▶ increased customer satisfaction
▶ faster decision making
▶ retained expertise
▶ increased communication
▶ shorter learning curves for new employees.

What are the main components of KM? (chapter 1)

▶ *People* are the main component. They contribute the majority of the knowledge, make use of it, and validate it or revise it based on their success with it.
▶ *Process* is the way the knowledge is organized and made available to the users. It becomes the communications vehicle that people use to find what they need.

▶ *Technology* includes the systems that are used to house, search, and maintain the knowledge. This may be software or hardware, internal or external, minimal or broad based; but it is a tool, rather than the end product, of knowledge management.

What are the basic steps I'll take to create a knowledge management system in my organization? (chapter 1)

1. Identify the internal (and possibly external) users of your knowledge management system.
2. Discover what knowledge the prospective users need to do their jobs and locate the sources of that information.
3. Determine the format or system that you will use to make this knowledge accessible to those who need it.
4. Confirm the gathered and captured information by circulating it to subject matter experts to correct, add to, and finalize.
5. Publish the knowledge in your KM system and teach the organization's members how to access it.
6. Initiate a feedback process and make revisions based on those responses and recommendations.
7. Maintain the system by creating ownership and regularly monitoring content and usage.

Why should my employees agree to use a KM system ? (chapter 2)

Because you show them that you use it. Be a role model in this. And because it will make their lives easier. If that's not incentive enough, it also helps if contributing to and using the KM system are some of the criteria judged in performance reviews.

Isn't this just more work? (chapter 2)

Initially, yes. But like all good programs, the implementation is proactive time spent, and eventual savings of time and effort will more than repay the initial outlay.

Your organization members also will find that many of the activities under the KM umbrella are things they're already doing. The KM system shares what they know and do with a larger group of people so that more value is generated by their daily efforts.

Isn't this the job of the training department? (chapter 2)

This is everyone's job. Unless knowledge management is enterprise-wide, it won't be used and maintained. Training departments certainly can help in promoting use of the system and teaching how to access the information contained there, but they can't be the sole owners of this process.

But gathering more data doesn't help if you don't know how to use the system that holds it, right? (chapter 9)

Yes, and that's why it's so important to teach all of your members how to use the KM system. It's also helpful if you offer examples to illustrate how the system and its contents will help them solve everyday problems.

Does this change people's job descriptions? (chapter 7)

Ideally, communicating and assisting team members have always been a part of your organization's culture, even if not specifically mentioned in job descriptions. It shouldn't be necessary to rewrite job responsibilities if your program demonstrates that this is a valuable tool rather than just another duty.

Won't it cause competition if I offer reward and recognition for contributions to the KM system? (chapter 4)

Not if you choose a recognition system that fits your organization's culture. If you see that a program of individual reward and recognition causes unhealthy competition, consider using team rewards or highlighting effective uses of the system without specific rewards attached.

If I'm planning a KM initiative next year, should I do my knowledge audit immediately? (chapter 3)

Please don't! There are few things as disheartening to an organization's members as participating in a survey, audit, or focus group on an initiative and not seeing any results for a long period of time. And needs change. You want to have the most recent facts reflected in your planning. It's a good idea to wait to conduct your knowledge audit until just before you begin your KM planning.

Where do I start? (chapter 3)

Start small in an area where you can make a quick impact on the organization. That will help you gain immediate results and support from users and management. Then add to the scope of the system once you've worked out the inevitable kinks.

Who can I get to help me with this? (chapter 1)

Create a KM system development team with representatives from across the organization. Each functional area has specific needs to address and results they'd like to get from the management of knowledge. You'll need to understand those diverse needs to design your system so it assists the largest population possible. And don't forget to enlist the support of management to ensure that the time and resources will be dedicated to making this initiative a reality.

How do I sustain this effort? (chapter 7)

Update, revise, and improve your system continually to satisfy the changing needs of the organization. Build in user recognition systems and highlight successes to maintain interest and encourage use of the system.

What are some of the biggest mistakes people have made in designing and implementing a KM system? (chapter 9)

A number of organizations have shared the fact that they invested in expensive and complicated technology before they had assessed what they needed in their KM systems. They ended up with enormous knowledge databases that were virtually unused. Other groups have started their projects on too large a scale, trying to address too many needs immediately. They had to scale back, which resulted in a lack of confidence in the system. Other challenges include a loss of focus that allows systems to stray from their central goals, KM teams and executives who don't model the knowledge-use behaviors they want their members to adopt and so encourage disinterest among employees, and a loss of attention by KM teams that permits outdated and incorrect information to be posted and accessed by members of the organization.

What happens if we don't do anything? (chapter 3)

Every time an employee walks out the door for the last time, she or he takes a wealth of knowledge along—knowledge that's developed over time and with experience, knowledge that may not exist in any other place. Furthermore, work will be duplicated and inconsistent procedures will continue.

Valuable lessons will benefit only those who experience them firsthand. And you'll continue to reinvent the wheel every single day.

If knowledge management is so important, why isn't everybody doing this? (chapter 2)

Because we live in a business world that operates mostly in the urgency mode, we work more often with a fix-the-crisis approach than with an approach of proactive planning. Organizations must be willing to step outside of their daily processes and consider the long-range impact of harnessing the knowledge in their midst before they'll realize the advantages of taking control of their knowledge assets by creating these KM systems. Many won't be willing to devote the time and resources needed to do this. It's a case of saving a nickel now to lose a dollar later.

How is this different from what we do now? (chapter 5)

Right now we have knowledge in our organizations. With management of that knowledge, we implement systems to circulate that knowledge and make more productive use of it. It's a more advanced communication system than what most organizations have used in the past.

How long do we have to keep doing this? (chapter 7)

Sorry, but this one never ends. Done successfully, knowledge management will become a part of your culture. When that shift occurs, trying to end it will prompt great weeping and wailing and rending of garments. Sorry, I got carried away there. The short answer is that knowledge management should become a permanent part of your business strategy.

What small steps can I take if I'm not ready to create a full-scale KM system? (chapter 9)

You can try the process by starting with the steps of knowledge management in a single department or area. Or begin by creating a master list of all the information resources that already exist and where they can be found. You can circulate the list and ask others to add to it. Then you can post this or circulate it to the organization as a reference tool. That's a low-tech knowledge-sharing system that will operate until you decide to develop a system that's more technology assisted. You could ask for submissions to a list of frequently asked questions and then circulate the list to get answered.

Have the accuracy and completeness of those answers confirmed, and then post the list on your intranet or put it in operations binders. Basically, any steps you take to begin identifying knowledge sources and sharing their information in your organization are good steps toward your future KM system.

What does a KM system look like? (chapter 8)

There's no single answer to this because it depends on your organization, its needs, and its resources. Ideally, it's a system that includes one gateway that leads users to all the resources they need, with a simple search feature to direct them to exactly what they're looking for. The sophistication of the portal and the knowledge base behind it may depend on many factors, including prospective users' level of comfort with technology, the development team's commitment to the technology that already exists in your organization, and of course, the budget. As KM practitioners, we have to be willing to let some initiatives stay informal—and just a little bit messy. Some communities of practice that operate well will lose their spontaneity and effectiveness if they're forced into a structured format. All told, a KM system is a combination of formal and informal knowledge networks. At any given time, some of the networks will be formatted and others will sprout organically.

Is there software to help me on this? (chapter 8)

Tons! The challenge is in sifting through the many available programs to find the one that best suits your needs and budget. Look at the guidelines in chapter 8 to get some idea of the features to look for and the questions to ask in selecting software that's right for your organization.

Remember that bigger is not always better. A software system that answers every possible need is not going to be useful to your organization if it's too difficult for people to understand or operate. The goal is not to create the biggest database of knowledge you can; it's to create a database that is used and updated often.

What's the difference between knowledge management and content management? (chapter 7)

Both knowledge management and content management systems deal with compiling, organizing, and circulating information. The difference is that content management focuses on data and information. It organizes files, projects, webpages, and other sources of information. Knowledge management focuses on the application of that data and information. Whereas content management systems will point a person to the document that contains information they need, a knowledge management system will connect that person with a community or expert who holds knowledge on how to use that information.

Should I use a consultant? (chapter 8)

Consultants can be helpful in creating the KM system. Outside assistance is not required, but sometimes it's useful to have someone who's been through this process successfully and can guide you around some of the common stumbling blocks. If you decide to retain the services of a consultant, contact other organizations to learn from their experiences; check the references of any consultants you're considering and look for a strong track record. For other specifics on what to ask and look for, review the suggestions in chapter 8.

My IT department will try to kill me over this, won't they? (chapter 5)

Very possibly. If they're like most information technology units, they're overloaded just trying to keep up with the technical needs of your organization. That's why you want to get them involved at the very beginning of the process, but not place the responsibility for developing and maintaining the system squarely on their shoulders. You need their input to ensure that you're being realistic in making plans for the system development and implementation, based on the current resources, technology, and personnel who are available to help in this undertaking.

Isn't all this social networking technology more directed to the younger generation? (chapter 9)

It's true that the generations who have grown up with computers in their homes are more comfortable with and adept at using online communication systems. But here's an interesting correlation: This same sort of social networking has been taking place as long as workplaces have existed. The difference is that the watercooler discussions have been replaced with blogs. The memos and project reports are being moved into wikis and online bulletin boards. And that one person in the office who knows where everything is can now be relieved of constant interruption because the system gateway and search features send seekers to those documents. Our task in this process is to make ourselves as comfortable talking with others through technology as we are talking with them at the watercooler.

What's in it for me? (chapter 2)

There are so many benefits for the people in an organization that uses effective KM systems. One of the biggest benefits is that you'll have the tools do your job more effectively, efficiently, and quickly. That means less frustration, less stress, and less wasted time.

Basic Rule 10

Ultimately, knowledge management isn't an exercise in managing. It's all about *communicating* the existing knowledge and expertise so that others can continue to build on that knowledge.

Why would I think about knowledge management for my customers? (chapter 9)

When you visit stores or businesses online and can find up-to-date and comprehensive information about the products for yourself, aren't you able to get answers and find what you're looking for more quickly? Aren't you able to compare services and prices and then make wise buying choices from a range of stores you'd never walk into? And what about the companies that post their product operating manuals or troubleshooting guides online? Don't they save you time and effort working with or fixing products you're using regularly? Those are the kinds of functions for which larger companies are using knowledge management. You also might consider using the KM system to resolve customer complaints and problems, to give your organization a 24/7 sales-and-service presence, and to let customers track orders. If any of those uses interest you and would benefit your customers, consider including a customer portal with password protection.

What if there are disagreements over information? (chapter 6)

There will be disagreements. Some processes are done differently and perhaps incorrectly across departments. You'll find inconsistencies in procedures, policy applications, and quality measures. But you know what? Those problems already exist and they're compromising your organization's performance and results. Creating a system that gathers and compares procedures, processes, policies, and reams of information will reveal those problems and open them to discussion and reconciliation. (I hope without too much bloodshed.) The outgrowth will be consistently high standards of practice throughout your organization.

Do you have questions to add to our frequently asked list? Visit http://www. KnowledgeManagementBasics.blogspot.com to post your questions and read other people's questions and answers. It's knowledge management in action.

Appendix B

Script for Your PowerPoint Presentation

■ ■

Here is a suggested script to accompany the PowerPoint slide presentation discussed in chapter 8. You can access the slides at http://www.astd.org/knowledgemanagementbasics.

Slide 1

I'd like to ask you a few questions:

1. Have you ever recreated something because it was easier than trying to find it?
2. Have you ever worked on a project and then found out someone else had already done something similar and could have saved you most of that work?
3. Have you ever said, "The person who does that isn't here today?"

All of those are symptoms. They show us that we have knowledge we aren't making the most of. Every day we're reinventing the wheel. And the process that can help us change that is knowledge management.

Slide 2

Knowledge management has been confused with software systems, online resources, intranets, and extranets—but those are just some of the tools of knowledge management.

When we talk about managing knowledge, we're actually talking about creating a system that helps us channel the knowledge in the organization to anyone who needs to access it.

That knowledge can be in all kinds of forms. It could be in documents, lists of lessons learned, or in the best practices of our managers. It could be those great connections and business relationships that our people have cultivated. It could be hiding in manuals and announcements that were forgotten long ago.

The way to coordinate this might include technology systems that let us link to all our documents from one central site. It can include communication systems and communities of practice in which people get together to share ideas. It basically can be as much or as little as we want to make it. But every step we take to organize the knowledge we have here is a step to make us more productive and profitable.

I'd like to give you an overview of knowledge management and what it involves.

Slide 3

There are three components of any knowledge management system.

1. The main component is *people*. In this system, our people are the ones who contribute the knowledge, review and confirm its accuracy and completeness, and use it in their work.
2. *Process* is whatever way we select to organize the knowledge and make it available to our users.
3. And *technology* is one of the ways we can make it easier to search and find the knowledge we need right when we need it.

Slide 4

What can knowledge management—also known as "KM"—do for us? One part of our business it can benefit is cost reduction. KM can help lower support costs by ensuring that information, including answers to frequently asked questions and guides for troubleshooting, are easy to access. It's an opportunity for us to develop an understanding of all the operations of our organization and analyze them so we can ensure we're being cost effective.

Slide 5

Another performance metric that knowledge management can help is productivity. By leveraging the expertise in our organization and applying what we learn in one area to work in another area, we become more productive. And as we create situations where people can be productive, we increase job satisfaction because most of us truly enjoy seeing the successful outcome of our efforts. That means increased retention of employees, so we hold onto that expertise and don't watch our valuable knowledge walk out the door.

Slide 6

Innovation. Only by knowing what we've tried before, what exists in our organization, and the benefit of the expertise that is everywhere in this company can we create an environment in which people aren't reinventing the wheel everyday. When we get past that stage, we've made it possible for our employees to move forward consistently with past experience to build on.

Slide 7

And finally, growth. When we're not spending time rediscovering the same information and losing knowledge, networks, and history every time an employee leaves, we've opened the door to unparalleled growth.

It basically comes down to the words of philosopher and aphorist George Santayana: "Those who cannot remember the past are doomed to repeat it." By keeping our history and the lessons learned accessible to all of us, we can ensure that we don't repeat past mistakes.

Slide 8

Let's take a look at the steps involved in creating a knowledge management system.

First is determining our needs. We'd want to assess where we are in our management of knowledge and what would help us most. Perhaps it's capturing the knowledge of our baby boomers who are getting ready to retire. Or it might be helping our customer service representatives quickly and fully access the information they need.

Slide 9

Then we begin discovering the knowledge sources that we have. We can start by seeing what exists in manuals, databases, checklists, directories, announcements, policies, calendars and schedules, and other documented forms of knowledge. Committed to paper or some other form of documents, that knowledge is called "explicit knowledge."

We'll also look for sources of "tacit knowledge." That's the kind of knowledge that comes from experience and relationships. We can learn a lot of this from our subject matter experts, those people who are specialists in certain areas of our operations.

Slide 10

Next we'll decide how to organize this information to make it easier for everyone to use. We'll choose the kind of system that will work best for the people in our organization. It may be anything from technology to improved face-to-face communication systems, or a combination of both.

Slide 11

Then we'll compile the knowledge that's available and send it to our experts to confirm or correct. At this point, we'll probably find some inconsistencies that we can reconcile and standardize, so we'll see some immediate benefits from this system. And we'll start circulating the information by letting people know that we've made it easier to get to the material they need.

Slide 12

Maintenance is a big ingredient in this system. If we don't continue to capture knowledge and to revise and update it regularly, the system won't be useful. That's where we give ownership to our experts. We place them in charge of their areas of expertise so that any information we have available to our employees is always the latest and the greatest.

Slide 13

What it all comes down to is that we, like progressive companies throughout the world today, know that the most valuable asset we have is our employees' knowledge. By creating a system that makes it easier to share that knowledge and build on it, we ensure that we don't have to learn the same lessons over again and that all the steps we take in the future expand and enhance our knowledge.

Slide 14

Questions?

Resources

Collison, Chris, and Geoff Parcell. 2004. *Learning to Fly: Practical Knowledge Management from Leading and Learning Organizations*. Chichester, West Sussex, U.K.: Capstone Publishing.

Dalkir, Kimiz. 2005. *Knowledge Management in Theory and Practice*. Burlington, MA: Elsevier Butterworth-Heinemann.

Davenport, Thomas H., and John Glaser. 2002. "Just-in-Time Delivery Comes to Knowledge Management." *Harvard Business Review,* 107–111.

Davenport, Thomas H., and Laurence Prusak. 2000. *Working Knowledge: How Organizations Manage What They Know*. Boston, MA: Harvard Business School Press.

Dixon, Nancy M. 2000. *Common Knowledge: How Companies Thrive by Sharing What They Know*. Boston, MA: Harvard Business School Press.

Drucker, Peter F., and others. 1998. *Harvard Business Review on Knowledge Management*. Boston, MA: Harvard Business School Press.

Edwards, John S., and Elayne Coakes. 2003. "Knowledge Management and Intellectual Capital." *Journal of the Operational Research Society* 54, 117–118.

Figallo, Cliff, and Nancy Rhine. 2002. *Building the Knowledge Management Network: Best Practices, Tools, and Techniques for Putting Conversation to Work*. New York: John Wiley & Sons.

Fountain, Darrell D. 2007. "Knowledge Management in an Information Age Army." USAWC Strategy Research Project. Carlisle Barracks, PA: U.S. Army War College. http://handle.dtic.mil/100.2/ADA469106 [accessed March 15, 2009].

Frappaolo, Carl. 2006. *Knowledge Management*. New York: John Wiley & Sons.

Fuller, Steve. 2002. *Knowledge Management Foundations*. Boston, MA: KMCI Press.

Groff, Todd R., and Thomas P. Jones. 2003. *Introduction to Knowledge Management: KM in Business*. Burlington, MA: Butterworth-Heinemann.

Headquarters, Department of the Army. 2008. *Field Manual*. Knowledge Management Section FM 6-01.1. Washington, D.C.: Headquarters, U.S. Army Training and Doctrine Command.

Jennex, Murray E. 2007. *Knowledge Management in Modern Organizations: Advances in Knowledge Management, Volume 1*. Hershey, PA: Idea Group Publishing.

Koenig, Michael E., and T. Kanti Srikantaiah. 2004. *Knowledge Management Lessons Learned: What Works and What Doesn't*. Medford, NJ: Information Today.

Mader, Stewart. 2008. *Wikipatterns*. Indianapolis, IN: Wiley.

Montano, Bonnie. 2004. *Innovations of Knowledge Management*. Hershey, PA: IRM Press.

Oakes, Kevin, and Raghavan Rengarajan. 2002. "E-Learning: The Hitchhiker's Guide to Knowledge Management." *T+D,* 75–77.

Paylow, K., A. Hickman, and D. Zappa. 2006. "Identifying Future Leaders Through Knowledge Management." *Journal of Petroleum Technology* 58 (10), 71–72.

Rao, Madanmohan. 2005. *Knowledge Management Tools and Techniques: Practitioners and Experts Evaluate KM Solutions*. Burlington, MA: Elsevier Butterworth-Heinemann.

Spector, J. Michael, and Gerald S. Edmonds. 2002. "Knowledge Management in Instructional Design." Syracuse, NY: ERIC Clearinghouse on Information and Technology, 2002. http://purl.access.gpo.gov/GPO/LPS42293 [accessed March 15, 2009].

Stankosky, Michael. 2005. *Creating the Discipline of Knowledge Management: The Latest in University Research*. Burlington, MA: Elsevier Butterworth-Heinemann.

Suresh, Hemamalini. 2002. "Knowledge Management: The Road Ahead for Success." PSG Institute of Management, Coimbatore, TN. http://www.providersedge.com/docs/km_articles/KM_-_The_Road_Ahead_for_Success.pdf [accessed March 15, 2009].

Svetlik, Ivan, and Eleni Stavrou-Costea. 2006. "Connecting Human Resources Management and Knowledge Management." *International Journal of Manpower* 28 (3-4), 197–206.

Wenger, Etienne, Richard McDermott, and William M. Snyder. 2002. *Cultivating Communities of Practice*. Boston, MA: Harvard Business School Press.

Knowledge Management Websites

http://www.apqc.org — American Productivity & Quality Center

http://www.brint.com/km — Brint Knowledge Management Network and WWW
   Virtual Library on Knowledge Management

http://www.chriscollison.com — Knowledgeable Ltd.

http://www.ejkm.com — Electronic Journal of Knowledge Management

http://www.entovation.com — Entovation International

http://www.groups.yahoo.com/group/act-km/ — Act-KM

http://www.gurteen.com — Gurteen Knowledge website

http://www.icasit.org/km — KMCentral

http://www.ikmagazine.com — *InsideKnowledge* Magazine

http://www.kikm.org — Kaieteur Institute for Knowledge Management

http://www.km4dev.org — KM for Development

http://www.kmci.org — Knowledge Management Consortium International

http://www.KMInstitute.org — Knowledge Management Institute

http://www.kmpro.org — Knowledge Management Professional Society

http://www.kmresource.com — Knowledge Management Resource Center

http://www.kmwiki.wikispaces.com — KMWiki

http://www.kmworld.com — *KMWorld* Magazine

http://www.knowledge-nurture.com — Buckman Laboratories International

http://www.knowledgeboard.com — KnowledgeBoard

http://www.knowledgebusiness.com — The KNOW Network

http://www.krii.com — Knowledge Research Institute

http://www.kwork.org — Association of Knowledgework

http://www.lucasmcdonnell.com — Knowledge Connects People

http://www.Skyrme.com — Knowledge Connections

http://www.vernaallee.com — Integral Performance Group

About the Author

Christee Gabour Atwood is a speaker, trainer, and knowledge management adviser who specializes in helping companies share the knowledge in their organizations. She has worked with corporations, associations, *Fortune* 500 companies, and government entities in analyzing, developing, and presenting programs to develop communication and leadership skills. She is the recipient of the 2006 Outstanding Adjunct Faculty Award at Baton Rouge Community College. Atwood's background includes radio personality, television host and anchor, and newspaper and magazine columnist. She also has served as executive director for state associations, editor/publisher of various trade and professional magazines, and CEO of The Communications Workshop, Inc. Atwood is a master facilitator for the Small Business Training Center in Baton Rouge, Louisiana, and has received training certifications from various organizations, including AchieveGlobal and Franklin Covey. And, because she believes humor is a vital part of effective communications, she also teaches "But UnSeriously Folks!"—a course on the effective use of humor in the workplace, which is based on the experiences in her humorous book, *Three Feet Under: Journal of a Midlife Crisis* (Book Republic Press, 2005). *Knowledge Management Basics* is Atwood's fourth book with ASTD Press. Her other ASTD Press titles are *Succession Planning* (2007), *Presentation Skills Training* (2008), and *Manager Skills Training* (2008). You may reach her at http://www.KnowledgeManagementBasics.blogspot.com.

Index